ENDOI

"Having known Gary King for decades, his book The Happiness Formula is a beautiful composite of who Gary is as a person. His wisdom perfectly represents how he 'walks the talk' and how to enhance your own life exponentially."

—Becky Robbins

"The Happiness Formula by Gary King contains a simple yet elegant formula for happiness. Emerging from years of growth work, both personal and professional, Mr. King distills happiness to the practices of forgiveness, truthfulness and self-worth. This leads to individuals who willingly choose to engage with integrity and honesty while ready to forgive self and others. That the subtle beauty of this prescription is authored by a man, who has experienced devastating suffering, is a testament to his resilience, courage and character."

—Frederic Luskin PhD.,

Author *Forgive For Good*, Director Stanford Forgiveness Projects

"I post many quotes from my friend and mentor Gary King. I'd like to share something personal with you in regards to WHY I'm so passionate about Gary's message. Since the age of 12 I've studied personal growth (thanks mom), and have been fascinated by what makes people successful and more importantly HAPPY. Well, with all the self-growth seminars, NLP trainings, hypnosis boot camps, and coaching I've invested in, no one has NAILED the TRUTH like Gary. It's IMPOSSIBLE to be happy if you are out of integrity. I was in a relationship that I knew wasn't right, and I lied to my friends, lied to my family, and lied to myself so I wouldn't have to change it. I was miserable. When I made the decision to be honest, forgave

myself, that's when everything changed. It wasn't some fancy NLP tool, it was good old fashioned HONESTY and FORGIVENESS. There's no way I'd have the giddy happy marriage I have today without that. Cheers to YOU being HAPPY!"

—**Mandy Keene**

"Gary King has created an absolute masterpiece. This book has the potential to be one of the greatest books of all time. Every teacher, CEO, politician, parent, banker and business owner MUST read this book."

—**Dave Albin**, *The Fear Whisperer*

"This book is captivating, insightful, empowering and reflective. I had trouble putting it down. Gary speaks from the heart. No ego, genuine, authentic, as the man himself. I shed many tears. This book is about Gary's life story: his pain, wins, loses and his mission to help others. He gives practical exercises, to help his readers take control of their lives. Gary expresses himself honestly and easy to understand. It is written by man who lives by his words. I highly recommend this book."

—**Christine Lee**, Sydney Australia

"Gary's work and message has constantly guided me both professionally and personally for over 2 decades now. I am grateful and lucky to have experienced the power of what he shares as it has benefitted my life in countless ways. Gary is in my top 10 list of who everyone should learn from. Please read his new book and see for yourself how your self-esteem, your relationships, your kids, your finances, your work and your overall happiness will shift dramatically!"

—**Ariane de Bonvoisin,**

Bestselling author, speaker, entrepreneur

"The Happiness Formula is raw and real wisdom. It reminds the reader that even though hard times happen, you choose what you learn from them. Valuable lessons from an amazing thought leader. I could not put it down, It should be a movie!"

—Loren Slocum Lahav,

Author of *The Greatest Love, Life Tune Ups, Chicken Soup for the Soul Time to Thrive*, international speaker, entrepreneur and mom

"Gary is heart, soul, mind and strength along with peace, joy, love and wisdom. He teaches without judgment and pours his wisdom and love into others in a practical and powerful way. My life and the lives that I expect to touch will forever be better, in no small part, because of the contributions of a man I am honored to call friend, Gary King, master of The Happiness Formula."

—Joseph Dalton

"THE HAPPINESS FORMULA by Gary King is a great guidebook for people facing challenges; whether they are challenges with health, finances or relationships. King's book is authentic, as he shares wisdom gleaned after making his own mistakes and blunders. Unlike books that simply share knowledge that has been re-packaged, King's insights were learned in "the school of hard knocks." Therefore, it is easy to follow his advice. His own journey is compelling, and readers will enjoy the book because King's life is filled with so much drama. When you see how he himself applied his solutions, and the results they brought him, others will quickly realize King's strategies can also apply to them."

—Tolly Burkan, Founder of the Global Firewalking Movement

"What sets Gary King apart from any other author or speaker is his unique ability to deliver real lasting change. His ideas stay with you and have a real and permanent impact on your life. Anyone looking for significant long term change and not a temporary band aid solution should look no further than Gary King."

—**Josh Panebianco,** Sydney, Australia

"Gary King is one of the most beautiful angelic souls I have encountered. Little did I know how close and how much impact our friendship would have in my life. His story, his astounding journey is now in the public domain and will help millions no doubt to understand how such a tragedy can work such miracles and strengthen the human spirit. It's been an honor and privilege to know you Gary. I cannot wait to read your book out on the 25th May, and see you again on its global launch and beyond. You are my hero, Gary."

—**Juliette MacVarish**

THE HAPPINESS FORMULA®

$F_2HT_2SW=HF^{10}$

The Ultimate Life Makeover™

Gary King

Published by Motivational Press, Inc.
1777 Aurora Road
Melbourne, Florida, 32935
www.MotivationalPress.com

Manufactured in the United States of America.

ISBN: 978-1-62865-295-6

Contents

FOREWARD

GARY KING'S JOURNEY OF BIG WINS AND HUGE LOSSES FAR EXCEED THE boundaries that most people can imagine. I met Gary in the early 90s and experienced the instant connection to the wisdom and compassion that he generously shares with others.

We spoke then about writing a book, and often since, unaware that the universe had so much more for him to endure and enjoy before it would be time.

The hours spent recording and reliving his journey were often emotional, occasionally painful, but always truthful. It has been my honor to play a role in sharing his message with the world.

Those of you fortunate enough to know Gary are aware of some of the incidents shared here. Those of you now joining Gary should prepare to understand the forgiveness, honesty, and truth that it took him and will take you to embrace, implement and arrive at true happiness.

The Ultimate Life Makeover is not a do-over. Your experiences create your uniqueness. Consider this book as an opportunity, a chance to achieve inner peace.

Enjoy the journey,

Vickie H Smith

ACKNOWLEDGMENTS

A VERY SPECIAL THANK YOU AND ACKNOWLEDGEMENT OF GRATITUDE to the following amazing people who made my speaker and author journey possible: They are truly precious treasures in my life.

Wayne Dyer and M Scott Peck, who started me on a life long journey of self-realization.

Oprah Winfrey, thank you for being an inspiration to the world. I am grateful you found my work worthy of publishing in "O" magazine and "O's Guide to Life" hard cover book.

Tony and Sage Robbins, who provided an international platform for me to add value, learn, grow, travel, and expand my horizons.

Vicki St. George, who invited me to give my first on stage presentation in The Gold Coast of Australia 15 years ago to 200 Anthony Robbins Leadership Training participants.

Ariane de Bonvoisin, a long time treasured friend, who has also provided me with endless publishing and media resources that have been priceless.

Lisa Rathmell Morgan, my Online Business Manager, who always goes over and above to create and manage the processes, operations and systems needed to run my business.

Loren Slocum and Jonathan Cardozo, who both believed in my message, and made it possible for me to grow and expand it to worldwide volunteer audiences.

Mary Glorfield, who made it possible 12 years ago for me to sell the "Pay Truth Forward" CDs at events, which contributed to a significant worldwide effect.

Ann McIndoo, who inspired, guided, encouraged and invited me to her "So You Want To Write a Book" programs, along with introductions to significant people in the media world.

Lizzi Luminati & Juliette MacVarish, who leveraged me to sign a commitment on a restaurant napkin in London to make this book happen. The napkin is framed and hanging on my office wall.

After my father's passing, it was an honor to take care of my mother, Jane Horton King, for 35 years. My dear friend Gary Lieberman, a host of my friends, and I built a custom home with separate living space for her and my Grandmother. It was a joy to take them both out of a modest home into a luxury one overlooking the water on Paradise Island. I miss her dearly; she always took amazing care of me.

Vickie Smith, who made it all happen by her personal commitment to support this journey. Her endless inspiration, unconditional love, amazing work ethic, constant support, and her never-ending vision of helping the world grow through the publication of this book. She took everyone listed above and wrapped them into a miracle package called *The Happiness Formula®, The Ultimate Life Makeover™*.

With gratitude,

Gary King

Treasured Souls

My life has been a journey of extreme pleasure and unimaginable pain shared within the following pages. A complete life is about people, not places and things. This list of treasured souls are some of the individuals that have added tremendous value to my life and shared part of their heart and soul with mine. I know I have forgotten to list a few of these treasured people, but only on this page, not in my heart.

Cindy Sistrunk, my son's mother, who gave so much love, courage, faith, patience, and understanding to our son. It is never fair when a child leaves before his parents. My prayers go out to her, as I know her prayers go out to me. We share a journey that is not for those without Faith.

Chris King Dewberry, my only sibling, my sister, she ran my marine business when it was amazing, and when my life completely imploded and fell apart. Together, we have endured the impossible. We have laughed, cried, fought, forgave, disconnected and reconnected. We took care of our mother, and took care of each other. Our Love is unconditional, even when there is distance, which is all part of growth.

Becky Robbins, Gary Wheeler, Johnny Green, Pattie Ferrentino King Crew, John Stross, Chuck Olson, Andy Ezekiel, Kathy Harmeling, Gerry and Mary Kirk, Bill Carl, George Orgera, Gini Grieb, Glen Smedley,

Butch Ellsworth, Gino Centanni, Christine Lee, Bobby Hoffman, Dave Jedlovec, Louie and Jini Pinto, Chuck Mellon, Clay Kelley, Bob Pickett, Louis Fujita, Jennifer Suns, Laurie Cossar, Dr. Richard Phares, Harry and Jean-ne Dent, Dr. Don and Sharon McLendon, Mary Beth Mittleman, Jill Blessing, Charity Beck, Bill Ganz, Billy Martin, Tolly Burkin, Pam & Doug Mayer, Pam Gibbons, Stan, Mandy and Jack Nickens, Liz Kern, John Messmore, Dave Albin, John Cox, Joseph McClendon III, Michelle Champine, Todd Spendley, Deb Battersby, Charles Hawkins, George Mitcheson, Butch Hensley, Glen Lechtanski, Sue Entwistle, Angie Rawlings Anderson, Pam Jacoby, Tom Nimon, Patrick Lewis, Laurie Minerd, Dave Coover, Jamie Greene, Michelle Soler, Dave Roberts, Ray Hanke, Mike Tackey, Georgia Abbate, Kelly Faith, Sue Talmadge, Richard and David Aaron, Alice White Hinckley, John Lenberg, Randy Rabe, Cello Russo, Susie Miller, Connie Vizaro, David Stoller, Rick Cramer, Chuck Olson, Kurt Johnson, Dr. Thomas Pettit, Dr. Theodore Mackler, Dr. Shay Roop, Dr. Bob Roop, Gary Lieberman, Michael Knight, The Brown Family, Jerry & Annie Rinker, Margaret Irving, Jan Avant, Kimberly Lea, Bunny Parsons, Jo Massaro, Kate Rittase, Patti Rondolino Hughes, Steve Prohlit, Gina and Joe Penell, Mark Ganguzza, Dr. Francis Butler, Dave Sanderson, Hal Taylor, Bill Keefe, Jim Dusel, Dr. Carol Bates, Captain Rick Hanson, Betsy Schott, Joe Nuzzo, Geraldine Nuzzo, Sister Ruth, Daystar Center, Everett Rice, Mike Bomar, Bob South, Gary Sullivan, Robin Egelston, Earl Cox, Justin Wasilkowski, George Pils, Drusilla Fuller Overwijk, Jason and Jenna Stross, Danny and Charlotte Walker, Noel Sams, Dave George, Brannon and Michelle Clark, Lisa Morgan, Karlson Strouse, John Sharfeld, Ted and Mary Macy, Rick Cicetti, Kim Johnson, Dawne Knudsen Riggs, Carrie Aaron, Dr. Jeff and Susan Audibert, Gary Spence, Tammy Tantilla, Miki Knowles, Joanne Chrobot, Paula Pecorella, Paul Julian, Billy Jannsch, Bonnie Prinse, Bob South, Steve Pentz, Kim Pentz, Kim Allen, Deidre McKeown, Maritza Duncan, Randy Henderson, Cat Wilson, Lizette LaForge, Lori Gagan, Paul Julian and Carlos Martin Martinez, Sarah Lyons, Amy Olis, Pam

Hendrickson, Evan Curtice, Dave Gould, James Ewing, the Mastery Family, the Dykens Family, Steve and Lee Stratton, Kytka Jezek, Zanna and Zynnia Jezek, Randee Hoffmier, Rita Wagner, Connie Copeland, Candy Wilson, Mark Robichaux, Diana Antonucci, Billy Cox, Georgette Elle, Frank and Peggy Eibell, Sarah, Michael and the Simon family, The Ferrentino family, Lyn Orns, Kathy Buckley, Charlie Gentry, Harry Singha, my nephew Tom Stock, Derek Dudinsky, Donya Diamond, Tom Martin, Liz Lita, Tad and Brenda Shinke, Jared Woodall, Rich Kuepper, Stevie Osterland and the City of St Petersburg Florida Special Events Team.

These people all touched my life in very specific ways. They rescued me, loved and helped me.

They added to the quality of my life and trusted me. They honored me by being my friend.

They served me and I served them, which is an honor in itself. They prayed for me. I laughed with them and cried with them. They all left me a better person for knowing them.

There are actually hundreds more names I could fill this book with to honor and thank. I apologize if you were not specifically mentioned. You are not forgotten.

DEDICATION

I DEDICATE THIS BOOK TO MY FATHER, WILLIAM JAMES KING WHO left early at 57 years old, and to my only son, Jason Allen King, who also left early at 40 years old. All my life with them, I wished to be their best friend. We all did our best. Unfortunately, that never happened. Both my father and my son gave me a gift. They taught me how to be my own best friend. I love and miss them both.

INTRODUCTION

THIS BOOK IS ABOUT LIFE: THE MIRACLE, THE MYSTERY AND THE challenges. It is about my life, my struggles and my self-actualization to create a formula to help others evolve from victim to victorious. Even though the context of our lives may differ, the emotions we experience are likely the same. We all search for Happiness although we have no definition other than what we have been taught academically, that success defines happiness. We have been conditioned to believe our academic education will serve us in our times of deep financial and emotional needs, but nothing could be further from the truth. We are masters of technology, victims of emotional reality, and deprived of a healthy emotional foundation.

Most humans search for miracles, focusing on financial, health and relationships. The majority search with no understanding of the mystery of life itself. Many people run from challenges, avoiding them as if they were punishment, potentially leading them to becoming a victim of learned helplessness, or worse, learned hopelessness.

Happiness is not a search or pursuit. It is an internal choice. You are about to learn the wisdom of choice and it will change your life forever. **It is never your circumstances that define your future and your destiny, it is your choices.**

Welcome to The Happiness Formula®, The Ultimate Life Makeover™.

Gary King

CHAPTER 1

IT ALWAYS BEGINS WITH CHILDHOOD

MY PHYSICAL BODY SHAKES. IF YOU TAKE A PUPPY AND ARE UNKIND enough to kick it or abuse it, it will cower and shake. That is what happened to me. I have had tremors my entire life, and people have made jokes about them saying things to me like, "Are you an alcoholic?" or "Do you have Parkinson's? Your hands shake all the time." No, I have tremors. My hands have shaken since I was five years old.

As a child, my friends were a boy who lived next door and a girl who lived across the street and we were all five-years-old. I lived in a house that backed up to a city park, and one afternoon, the three of us were together there and decided we were going to play doctor. The whole idea was that the little girl was going to lay face down, and she was going to pull her pants down, which is what happened, no more, no less.

Afterward, the little girl went home and told her parents. When her parents contacted my father, he proceeded to drag me across the street to their house and subjected me to what would be considered a horrific shaming in front of this girl's parents. I do not have memory of what he actually said, or the details of his shaming me, which is not unusual as people will sometimes bury traumatic memories in a false sense of self-preservation, but I do have a memory of how I felt during the incident. I experienced emotional trauma equivalent to an animal beaten so that it cowers and shakes. I started having tremors then, and still do to this day.

At five years old, was I doing something that was radically inappropriate? Not at all. Not every child engages in that behavior, but many do because children are curious. Five year old children don't have cognitive skills. They are not thinking the way parents think. Whatever it was my father did, and for whatever the reason he did it, I suppose it had to do with making me wrong so that he would not have to be wrong as a parent. Nonetheless, it traumatized me, and I remember it to this day. What happens in your childhood can often stay with you throughout your lifetime.

In addition, I was born with a rather large birthmark on my left cheek the size of a penny. As a child with a very small head, that birthmark might as well have been 6 inches in diameter! When I looked in the mirror, all I saw was the mole and it was traumatizing. In my mind, the mole was an indicator that I was unattractive; that I was a malfunction, and there was something wrong with me because I had a mole on my face. Children can be ruthless, and when I was eleven my best friend constantly made fun of me, even calling me "Mole".

When I was 37 years old, the mole that had traumatized me my whole life changed shape. After examining it, the plastic surgeon confirmed it was deformed, and needed to take a biopsy and remove it. I was uncertain. I couldn't agree to have the mole removed, and had to go home and decide, puzzled as to why I thought there was even a decision to make.

The very thing that caused me to feel ugly would be gone! The plastic surgeon assured me there would be no scar – no sign of that birthmark on my face. So why did it take me two weeks to decide? Why wasn't I able to say, "Take it off right now"?

I had become addicted to the pain of seeing myself as ugly because of the mole. I had actually created a *relationship* with the mole, and created a relationship with "ugly". It was part of my identity, even though that identity was negative. It was an outpatient surgery, and the doctor took a syringe and injected the painkiller right into the center of the mole, which was excruciatingly painful. He gave me the injection and came back 15 minutes later to proceed. To remove the mole and not have a scar, he had to make a three-inch incision, starting at the bottom of my eye to fold the skin together. He began to make the incision, only to find out that the pain medicine injection never took. He gave me another shot and then proceeded.

I look back at it now and understand why the first injection didn't take. I had projected so much pain into that area of my body that the shot didn't even work. I left the office with the whole left side of my face bandaged. At the time, I was sponsoring a women's softball team. I went from the actual surgery directly to the playing field. I remember walking into the dugout, and all the players ran up to me saying, "What happened to you? Did you get in a car accident?"

I said, "No, I had my birthmark removed." They all looked at me saying, "What birthmark?" It gave me an epiphany. I spent my life from 5 to 37 years old beating myself to a pulp because I had a mole on my face that no one even noticed. One of the girls came in from the outfield, looked at me and said, "Tell me you did not have your birthmark removed. I would have paid to have that on my face." Even though the mole was removed, I still saw myself as ugly for 20 more years.

My life experiences have shown that what people go through in their childhood is often the source of self-worth issues. In my lifetime, I have seen countless female friends go through very expensive plastic surgery procedures, altering their body in numerous ways thinking it will change them emotionally if they spend the money.

Personally, I don't know any woman that has ever had an emotional self-worth shift from plastic surgery. It noticeably changed their body, but it did not noticeably change their self-worth. Their insecurities remained. I understand the quest because I had gone through the same thing. I did it, and it didn't change me at all. The trauma from the mole was no longer a trauma, however removing the mole did not increase my self-worth.

Chapter 2

STACKING THE TRAUMA

If you have experienced trauma as a child, you unconsciously move forward matching up your life experiences to the original cause. If your original cause is thinking, "I'm bad, wrong, ugly, at fault, or there's something wrong with me", then you go out into the world and unconsciously look for things that match those thoughts because you're trying to prove that you are right.

Most people don't go out into the world and try to prove themselves wrong. When it comes to having low self-worth, they are unconsciously looking for matches. They are looking for a match that validates that they are not enough, and not whole. All the way through school, it showed up in a multitude of different ways.

I graduated high school right before my 17th birthday. We had been to the graduation ceremony, and I was in a car headed to a party with a friend of mine. We were following another good friend driving his Harley Davidson. There was a half mile long straight stretch of road, and he looked back to make sure we were behind him. He ran into the back of a parked Jeep and died instantly. That was my high school graduation day.

A few days later, I turned 17 and went to work as a mechanic. I had an income, and very little overhead because I lived at home with my parents. I bought a 63.5 Ford convertible. A few months after graduation, some friends of mine had a very small party at their house. There were only ten people there; five guys and five girls.

I was sitting in a recliner watching television when all of a sudden the front door came off the hinges. Five guys had kicked the door down, and three of them jumped on me. I didn't even know who they were.

I didn't have the opportunity to get out of the chair. They beat me unconscious and continued to beat me after I was unconscious. I remember I came to, hearing a lot of screaming. I was face down on the floor and I was slapping all around with my hands. Everything around me was soaking wet. Both of my eyes were so badly beaten; they were swollen completely shut, so that I could not see. Finally, a screaming woman came over to me and wiped one of my eyes. From what I could barely see, I was on the living room floor right by the chair. All the slapping around I had been doing was my own blood. An ambulance took me to the hospital, suffering right brain damage due to the severe head trauma. I continued to stack emotional trauma on top of the physical trauma.

When I was 22 years old, I developed rheumatoid arthritis, which is very unusual as it usually happens later in life. Why did I have rheumatoid arthritis at 22? Because it is driven by emotional patterns; and I was an emotional mess. I had less than zero self-worth.

The day before my 26th birthday, one of my closest friends came to chat with me and he was in fear for his life for a multitude of reasons. The next morning, his body washed up on the beach. He was 21 years old, and there was never a definitive answer about what exactly happened to him. It was another emotional blow to me because one of my closest friends lost his life on my birthday.

If like me, you had no knowledge about the stages of grief and loss, you don't know how to manage it. If you keep going through these patterns, with no emotional skills and no quality emotional support system, these emotions stack on top of each other over time. That is why it is referred to as the "stacking effect". It affects you consciously, and when it ekes its way into your subconscious mind, it becomes a pattern that's extremely difficult to alter. Managing your subconscious mind with your conscious mind requires great skill.

When I started in grief counseling, I learned there are five steps you go through in grief. Denial, anger, "I should have, I could have, Why didn't I?" (bargaining), depression and acceptance.

At the time, I didn't recognize the cycle and found myself getting stuck for years, unable to move forward through the stages. I personally know people who have been stuck in denial, anger or depression, unable to move forward towards acceptance after going through horrific grief. Has this happened to you or someone you know? I highly recommend grief counseling so that a trained therapist can help guide you through the process.

CHAPTER 3

SILENTLY SCREAMING

I NEVER HAD A RELATIONSHIP WITH MY FATHER. I RECALL ONE TIME he carried me on his shoulders into a barbershop when I was four years old. When I was six years old, I remember he was digging something in the backyard with a shovel and I went next door to borrow a shovel to dig with him. Those two instances are the only times I can remember having any connection to him at all.

When I was 20 years old, I came home about 1:00 in the morning and noticed my mother's car was not in the driveway. I went inside and found a note on the kitchen table that said, "Your father had a heart attack and he's in the hospital." The next morning my mother told me what happened and for the next five or six days, she told me, "You have to visit him." I kept saying, "Absolutely not. I will not visit him. He doesn't even like me." Finally, on Mother's Day, to please her I went to see him. He was due to get out of the hospital in two days. I was at the foot of his bed, and in the first a minute of small talk, he took a deep breath, his eyes rolled back in his head and he died. The nurses ran in and shoved me out of the room, calling out "Code Blue! Code Blue!" I went to a pay phone and called my mother to tell her he'd died.

I felt certain that my presence gave him a heart attack simply because I walked in the hospital, and I cried for ten days straight. At his funeral, I heard family whispering, "We don't understand why Gary's so upset. He was never really connected to his father." The truth of it was very different: "Gary is upset. He never felt connected to his father, and now his father's gone, and he can't repair the lack of connection."

I never had a quality emotional support system that could have helped me with my grief and feelings of guilt. This is not a criticism of my family. They lacked understanding and life skills to help me, so they just ignored it.

I'll never know why my father died within minutes of my arrival, but here's what I believe: I believe my father was silently screaming "please love me, please love me," so loudly that I couldn't hear him. At the same time I was silently screaming back, "Dad, please love me. Please love me," so loudly that he couldn't hear me. That was the way it was between us.

Sadly, it was the same between my son and me, as well as with my father and his father. I noticed my father was not connected to his own father. I don't ever remember my father hugging me. Do I ever remember my mother hugging me? Perhaps only five or six times in my lifetime. Because of the amount of guilt I had thinking I'd killed my father, I took care of my mother, moving her into my house for 35 years until the day she died.

In my office, there is a picture of my father, and I cannot relate to his image in any way. It could be a picture of any person. I have pictures of my mother and my grandmother, and of course, I recognize who they are, but when I look at my father's picture, I can't even remember seeing his face.

Chapter 4

THE FIRST SPARK OF FORGIVENESS

I MARRIED AT 30 YEARS OLD WHICH I JOKINGLY SAY IS LATE IN LIFE because most of my friends married in their early 20s. I had gone through a series of failed relationships because as far back as I can remember; I felt the main purpose of a relationship for me was validation. That need for validation was the reason why I entered into a relationship.

I would want to be in a relationship with any female who would validate me, like me, love me or value me. When the foundation of a relationship is to get somebody to accept you, like you, love you, validate you, treasure you, idolize you, you are in trouble from the start because it rarely works. If you don't know how to validate yourself, like yourself or value yourself, you won't find that validation from someone else.

Did I ever get a relationship to work? Was I able to be part of a thriving, growing, fulfilling relationship? No, I never did, and at the time, I could not understand why.

My marriage lasted seven years, and it did not work. It wasn't sustainable for a myriad of reasons, but my low self-worth was the main reason why. Another was that I was trying to be in a relationship and not in a relationship simultaneously. During my seven-year marriage,

I had three affairs. The sad thing about the affairs is they had nothing to do with my wife. They had nothing to do what she provided or didn't provide to me and our marriage. They had to do solely with my insecurities.

My wife divorced me in 1984, and I took on the role of the rejected party, the abandoned party, the hurt party. So what did I do? What do many people do when another hurts them? Seek revenge. I decided I was going to get even. I was going to play the sandbox game: You hurt me, so I'll hurt you worse, and that's what I did. I hired a well-known attorney who was ruthless.

For a year, I danced the divorce routine that people go through and all the damage it causes. We did not have a child in our marriage so that wasn't a factor. I spent a lot of money on the attorney, spent money on a private detective, and the subpoenas were flying. It was just a big circus.

I had been in this ego maniac mindset of getting even no matter what it cost for the past year, and on an early Saturday morning, I was lying in bed when something came over me. I picked up the phone to call my attorney and said, "I've changed my mind. I want you to give my wife everything she asks for in the divorce."

His response to this sudden change of events was to say, "Are you crazy?! We go to court on Monday. You will owe her nothing when court is over." I said, "Let me repeat myself. I want you to give her everything she asked for in the original set of papers. The amount of money and all the items she demanded. I want her to have every single thing listed. End of story." He was irate.

I've often told this story to people going through a divorce, and also that it was one of the best decisions I had ever made in the all years I've been on this planet. Why? Because that decision came from a spark of self-worth, a spark of forgiveness that I'd never experienced before. It was a spark of character, ethics and integrity. I knew who I was in the marriage, and I knew who she was in the marriage. There was nothing to hide. I knew the right thing to do, and I knew the damaging thing to do. I did the right thing.

I know many people who have gone through divorce, who, regardless of financial status, end up with collateral damage that in some cases are irreversible and irreparable. The sort of collateral damage that's caused when you decide that love no longer exists and revenge does. I know many people that have paid $500,000 or more for attorneys to prove a point or to get even emotionally. For those who have done that:

» Can you reverse the emotional damage?

» Can you reverse the emotional damage you're doing to yourself?

» Can you reverse the emotional damage to your children?

» Can you reverse the emotional damage to the other person?

When you attack the other person, you are also attacking yourself. You just don't realize it at the time.

If you are prone to revenge, remember the old saying that goes, "If you seek revenge, dig two graves: one for the other person and one for you." You aren't just damaging the other person, you are damaging yourself in the process by expending energy in anger, deceit, deception and dishonesty. It takes that kind of negative energy to engineer that kind of situation.

Here's the reality check: If there are children involved, the last thing you want to do is pour all that negative energy onto the situation, because you can cause irreversible and irreparable damage to your children.

Turning the breakup of someone you took vows with or had children with into a Super Bowl of damage often leaves children wondering if they were a factor in the divorce. I've had parents tell me, "Oh my God! I found out years after the fact that my child considered suicide because they thought one of the reasons for our pending divorce was because of them."

When I delivered my mother's eulogy, my ex-wife Patty was sitting in the front row. I announced to the full house, "This is my ex-wife, Patty. I was married to her for seven years, and I did not deserve her." That was a statement of fact, and I made a public announcement to that effect. She was a great wife. I was not a great husband. I couldn't be.

When you have no quality emotional support system, you tend to look for emotional support anywhere you can find it. After the divorce, the depth of my insecurity and low self-worth was at such a level that I believed I had to immediately find somebody else to like me.

I was alone at home after being married for seven years, and I had to call up a female friend of mine and ask her to come and sleep in the same bed with me. It had nothing whatsoever to do with physical intimacy. I needed her to come and sleep in the same bed with me much like a little child would want to sleep in the same bed with their parents. I was a professional race boat driver. I owned a high profile business, but at 38 years old, I could not sleep alone in bed at night. Can you imagine how that felt? That's how twisted it was. I know I am not the only human being on planet earth that went through experiences like that. There's no shortage of people who are relationship jumpers because they cannot be by themselves.

Being alone and being lonely are two very different things. I have no issues with being alone. Lonely is a huge challenge, especially when driven by horrible insecurity. I was also shouldering immense guilt, crippling insecurity and huge ugliness.

My research tells me that currently there are more insecure, low self-worth people than high self-worth secure people. On the low side, I'd say the ratio is likely 90/10, but it probably closer to 98/2. I imagine that's because that's the way the game of life is set up. The game is set up through the educational process to not understand who we are as human beings. We certainly aren't given the benefit of healthy emotional skills at birth. It is a constant process of trial and error until you understand the framework, the foundation and the traits of healthy self-worth.

Chapter 5

THE DEATH RATTLE

After the divorce, I immediately jumped into a relationship with a woman who turned out to be an alcoholic. When that also ended, I was so despondent that I couldn't leave my home. I was too afraid to walk out of my front door, and found a safe haven on my couch. The only environment I could fully control was my couch; anything more than that would cause me to have a PTSD attack. I felt I could not control anything else, I couldn't control what people would say to me, or if they would like or not like me, so I stayed within the confines of my house.

I had lost 45 pounds, and to those who knew me, I appeared very sick. I was so depressed that I went upstairs, lay on my bed, and *knew* I was going to die. I don't know how to describe how it felt; my body rattled as if it was coming undone and it felt like whatever life force that holds everything together was starting to leave my body.

While lying on my bed, I came out of my body and went up to the corner ceiling of my bedroom. It is a strange sensation when you realize you've spent your life thinking the thing you consider you is somehow your physical body. You, the person, the personality, the consciousness, whatever you want to call it, is one and the same with the body. I discovered that isn't true because I was up at the ceiling, my consciousness or whatever you want to call it was disconnected from the body, and I was looking down at myself. I was looking down at nothing. In other words, I saw myself lying on the bed and I looked disgusting and emaciated. I could look around, look out of the windows, I could hear, and I was fully conscious. The "me" had nothing whatsoever to do with my body. It was a completely separate entity.

I did not go into a tunnel and see a white light or anything like that, but I was completely separate from my physical body. I don't know how long this went on. I just know it was long enough to make a lot of conscious observations before suddenly snapping back into my body. If I had to guess, I'd say I was less than a minute from physically dying.

Let me say that my relaying this experience is not about altering anyone's belief systems. I am merely recounting my life experience, which has been a great help to me over the last 14 years. I conduct a tremendous number of interventions with people from all over the world, so this experience has helped me relate to what life is.

When I snapped back into my body, I discovered a very interesting thing.

I could not lie.

Prior to this experience, I was not a pathological liar. I was basically honest, but you cannot be an honest person and have adulterous affairs. I participated in what I would have called, and will call "normal behavior". When I had this near-death experience, I found I could no longer lie in any way, and it was a real struggle for the first few months. Something radically shifted.

In many ways, it felt like I had the innocence and curiosity of a child again, and everything was fascinating. Looking at trees, feeling a breeze, it was all as if it was the first time. There was a point in which I was so acutely conscious, and so acutely aware that I could sense what people were going to say before they said it.

I searched to figure out how this could have happened and found that going through an enormous shift of consciousness in a very short time period is very unusual. Typically, these shifts in consciousness occur over a long period of time. You may have heard stories of those in their final hours becoming acutely conscious, suddenly discovering all the things they thought were paths to happiness and fulfillment were actually the opposite. Sadly, they discover it when it's too late to do anything about it.

Often when one has a huge shift in consciousness, they achieve clarity in aspects of their life, but once they integrate back into normal life, they often lose part of the acute awareness they had, and fall back into the same rut. One degree at a time, they will fall back into patterns that do not serve them, which is what happened to me. As long as I stayed acutely aware and was still in the acute awareness stage, I was fine.

Over the next three or four years, once that acute awareness faded, I fell back into being influenced by my surroundings instead of being the influencer. It's very easy to do.

If one isn't careful, they can fall into the influence that changes your behaviors without realizing it is happening. Why? Even though I was acutely aware of the lying part, I had not researched and dealt with my self-worth issues. So even though I had an acute awareness around ethics and integrity, I didn't have the acute awareness about self-worth. That developed later.

Having this near-death experience has helped me enormously in conducting interventions with people. I receive many calls from distraught people who are ready to take their life. I receive even more calls from someone with a close friend or relative ready to take their life and they want me to call that person, or they want to talk to me about the fact that they want to leave. I tell them from my life experience, I am going to ask some questions.

The first question I ask is, "Do you want to get out of pain? Or do you want to leave?" If they want to get out of pain, I can tell them exactly how to do that because I have done it myself. If they want to leave, I ask where they got the idea that doing something to their physical body will take them out of their pain, telling them, "Your body and who YOU are, are separate things. If you desecrate your body, if you break it, the consciousness that is YOU comes out and wanders around." I tell them it happened to me, so act accordingly. If they want to get out of pain, I will help them. I routinely assist people in getting to a therapist if they can't afford it because I know what it feels like to be drowning without resources.

CHAPTER 6

I RESCUED A WOMAN, AGAIN AND AGAIN

WHAT STARTED OUT AS AN INNOCENT BLIND DATE, CONSEQUENTLY turned into a 27 year, blindsided, roller coaster ride. From the start, my intuition warned me something wasn't quite right. I was not feeling particularly attracted to her and felt she had a dark cloud following her. In one of our first meetings, I was behind her car at a traffic light when a car broadsided her. She spent the night in the hospital, while I sat in the waiting room until sunrise waiting for her to be released. From then on, I felt compassion and the strangest obligation to rescue this woman from a series of never ending crisis stories. After a few dates, we were in a romantic relationship. After she had been evicted from her roommate's apartment, she and her young daughter moved back in with her parents, because she no longer had transportation.

This was the beginning of the rescue missions. I offered her and her daughter to move in with me and took on the responsibility of taking care of them. One day, after almost a year together, she started an argument with me about nothing really, and announced that she and her daughter were moving out. She moved that very night only six blocks from me, with another man who was a deceitful acquaintance of mine.

Nine days later, I was in complete shock as she married him.

I felt abandoned. I became so despondent and depressed I couldn't function. At one point, I was in such enormous pain and suffering, I made a critical decision. I headed for the kitchen, stood over the sink, took a serrated steak knife and put it to my wrist, seconds from ending it all. As I started the process, I realized I did not have the courage to end my life, and I didn't have the courage to live it either. The actual motive behind the choice to end my life was twofold; to get out of the intense emotional pain I was feeling, and to hopefully put the woman into deep emotional pain to get even with her for purposefully hurting me. This is unfortunately a situation that is all too common, a permanent solution to a temporary problem.

My friend George Mitcheson came to my house and ultimately saved my life. He convinced me to go to a presentation in Orlando, Florida given by a well-known personal development speaker, Tony Robbins. It took him more than a week to convince me to go, and I was so depressed I had to meet with a hypnotherapist before I could make the 80-mile drive.

While at the presentation, I purchased a ticket to a four-day program offered that was occurring the next month. During that event, I made a decision to implement dramatic changes in my life, and became part of a group of volunteers who ran the events, later becoming a subcontractor.

Before my self-imposed isolation, I was a marine mechanic with several employees. I worked hard and played hard, dividing my life between being a workaholic and going to the local bar/pub connecting with friends. When I made the choice to make dramatic changes, all that changed and I felt like I was on the mend.

Several months later, the woman called as if nothing had ever happened between us and told me she was getting a divorce because her husband was abusing her in a multitude of ways. She also said she was pregnant, and the child was mine.

I was at the hospital when the baby girl was born, premature. Her mother was insistent that I sign the birth certificate, but I declined because I had reason to believe she was not authentic with regard to paternity. For several months following the baby's birth, she moved in with a female friend of mine, and for the next 18 months, I cared for her daughter, even taking her to work with me. For a short period, I allowed them to move back in with me, as I felt obligated to help her.

While the woman was preparing to divorce her husband, she found she needed to establish paternity to proceed. She asked me to take and pay for a DNA test, and I complied. It was negative. The child was not my biological daughter.

At that point, she took the child out of my life, immediately moved to the other coast of Florida, and resumed a relationship with the estranged father of her older daughter. She later became pregnant again by the same man.

I was abandoned again.

Her leaving me again coupled with the loss of the child threw me back into clinical depression, and triggered a year and a half of PTSD. I sadly found myself spiraling back into suicidal thoughts, finding seclusion to be my only safe haven. I ignored my business, thankful that my sister managed and took care of it in my absence.

At one point, I spoke with an intuitive friend, Mary Ann Ford, and when I told her what happened, she said, "Gary, you are treating this like it is a punishment. The reality is it is a gift that this woman is out of your life."

I didn't have direct contact with the woman for several years, but was told she had married for a third time, divorced and married again. I briefly saw her daughter when she was eight years old, but I would only hear from the woman when she was in overwhelm and needed emotional or financial support.

One day she called saying she wanted to change her life, and wanted a free ticket to attend a personal development seminar that I was working at. I secured a ticket for her, and made the discovery that this was not about her changing her life, but about getting back into mine.

I started dating her again, and after a few months, she once again asked me to let her move into my house. I made it clear that was not an option, and I was no longer into rescuing her and saving her from herself. She became quite upset with me, and I did not communicate with her for quite some time afterward.

During this time of non-communication, her daughter, who was now 14 years old, called and asked me to be her father. After much contemplation, and once again the familiar feeling of obligation and compassion, I verbally agreed but did not formally adopt her. I no sooner agreed, when there began an ongoing barrage of phone calls with every imaginable crisis from dysfunctional boyfriends to a constant stream of emotional, financial and physical traumas, including asking me to co-sign a $55,000 college loan. The intuition I had ignored proved correct again. I understood this was just another manipulation tactic to get financial and emotional support.

Her mother and I remained friends, but her communication with me was sporadic, only coming when she or her daughter needed something. She manipulated me into sharing myself with her daughter, and her actions played a part in the disconnection with my own biological son.

I continued irregular visits with the girl I referred to as "my daughter". She would appear with short notice, almost always with a situation she needed help to resolve. Her relationship with her mother appeared to be extremely dysfunctional, aggressive and plagued with verbal confrontations and an over-abundance of profanity and the silent treatment.

During one of the "off again" periods, I got a call from the woman, who now lived 90 miles away. Her unemployment had run out and she had been living in her sister's home with her mother who had just passed away. Her sister evicted her within days of their mother's passing, which is a strange circumstance to say the least. She asked me to look for an apartment for her in the city I lived in, provided me with a list of addresses to look at, and after checking, I determined them to be unsuitable. She asked if she could move in to the other side of my residence and rent from me. I should mention my residence is unique in that although it is a single family home, it has a separate section I built for my mother to live in. There hadn't been anybody in that part of the residence since my mother passed away eight years prior.

I ignored my past relationship with her, and decided it would be nice to have companionship at that stage of my life. I had absolutely no intention of pursuing a romantic relationship with her, but I felt obligated and driven by my conscience to help her, a decision that became the ultimate nightmare.

I agreed to let her move in, rent-free. We agreed to try the arrangement for one month, and if it didn't work, then she would find another place to live. For the first four months, it was wonderful and she was exceptionally charming. Though it was not my intention to get into another romantic relationship with her, against my better judgment I found myself attracted to her emotional charm, not realizing it was a game to her.

Then the façade ended, and her behavior became radical, her lies unbelievably bold. She had become so manipulative she appeared to believe her pathological far-fetched nonsense. She would go from charming to road rage in two seconds, and it became clear she had serious clinical, mental challenges that had escalated over time.

Throughout our friendship/relationship, she only contacted me when she had a trauma or crisis going on in her life, and her interest in me was always about fulfilling a financial need: an unpaid electric bill or any other financial short fall. I became her "ATM", Any Time Money. I was known as a "Mr. Fix-it" type person, whether it was with regard to physical things, or as it pertained to human beings I could rescue or enable, or more importantly, be compassionate, kind and operate from my conscious. At no time did she ever assume personal accountability for her actions, I assumed due to low self-worth and lack of emotional availability. At that point, I didn't realize the real source of her dysfunction.

Against my will and permission, she allowed her daughter (the one I'd previously considered mine), and her daughter's boyfriend to move into my home with her. Though I told her I did not want them to live there; she moved them in anyway saying they were only to be there for a couple of weeks. Six months later, they were still living in my home, rent-free.

It had become crystal clear she was purposefully and consciously triggering my long term PTSD. Often, I had asked them to read, or at least research the symptoms of triggering PTSD, but they chose not to. I knew I had to end the relationship completely, and concluded that she, her daughter, and the daughter's boyfriend had to be evicted from my home.

One night, she started an argument, which resulted in my telling her she had to leave my house immediately. She did not comply, and I had to move out of my own home for four nights in an attempt to avoid a PTSD attack – unsuccessfully. She stayed six more days, then finally all three left, owing me a sizable amount of money in personal loans.

I had allowed myself to be manipulated, deceived, dangerously verbally and mentally abused, and stolen from by those who had no conscience or compassion for far too long. Their intentionally cruel actions caused me to file a police report against them. As far as I know, they appear to have gone on their merry way to yet another group of victims.

My strong "conscience", courage and compassion guided me through this unimaginable 27-year ordeal. To live with someone who has a selective, or zero conscious is not living. It is pure manipulation to feed self-absorption.

In retrospect, I realize she had always exploited my "blind side", looking for my emotional vulnerability. My discovery was that I was only trying to heal the childhood damage between my father and I, which had been buried in my subconscious for years. I tried to get her to love and like me, just as I had wanted my father to do. The irony is, sociopaths cannot love or be loved. It is impossible. For me it was "Mission Impossible", a lifestyle I embraced – Give me a challenge, I will "fix" it.

To this day, many of her past husbands, lovers and employers have communicated to me that they do not even want to hear her name as it triggers layers of trauma, episodes of PTSD, anger, anxiety and disgust.

Out of my conscious wish that others not endure a similar nightmare, I offer this advice: Stay away from those who constantly play the "pity card". That can very well be the telltale sign of complicated mental disorders.

Understand the symptoms of what could very well be serious mental illness:

1. Failure to conform to social norms
2. Deceitfulness and manipulation
3. Impulsivity, inconsistency and failure to plan ahead
4. Irritability and aggressiveness
5. Reckless disregard for safety of self and others
6. Consistent irresponsibility
7. Lack of remorse after having hurt, mistreated, or stolen from another person

When it comes to your friendship and relationship choices, a modified adage holds true: "If it looks like a fish, swims like a fish and smells like a fish, it is a fish, or a sociopath?"

CHAPTER 7

ACCIDENTAL ANGEL

ONE AFTERNOON A FRIEND CALLED AND ASKED ME TO PICK UP A starter for his car in downtown St. Petersburg. There are two major roads in and out of downtown; First Avenue South, a five lane road heading into downtown and First Avenue North, another five lane road heading out of downtown.

It was about 2 o'clock in the afternoon, and I was traveling down First Avenue South in the center lane of five and the street was busy with traffic. Suddenly there was a tremendous crash of something hitting my truck. I heard screams and pulled over to the curb having no idea what had just happened.

Witnesses said a woman with three children holding hands was in the middle of the city block when they started to cross the street, not at an intersection, nor crosswalk; the middle of the block. When they were nearly to the center lane, she panicked because traffic was moving faster than she thought. She turned loose of her children and told them to run.

I ran over her five-year-old boy and killed him instantly. I laid on my front seat, in utter shock. My driver's door was open and a man approached me yelling and screaming that I'd just killed his son and he was going to kill me. The police and ambulance arrived, and the police interviewed me as well as the witnesses. I was not charged, nor ticketed for the accident.

As I went home, I remember thinking about how I had made so much progress, and now I had slipped further back than I was at my worst. I had inadvertently just been part of taking a child's life.

The next morning my doorbell rang and found a man standing there in a suit. He asked if I were Gary King as he was handing me his business card. He was an attorney, one commonly referred to as an ambulance chaser. He asked me if my house and business were owned free and clear, and I closed the door in his face, thinking how cold, cruel, and heartless human beings can be.

I wanted to pay for the funeral for the boy, so I began searching for information and learned his family was homeless, street people. I went to the Day Star Center, a shelter located at the time in a little wooden building behind the Catholic Church in downtown St. Petersburg run by a Sister Ruth. It operated by donation. Sister Ruth knew the boy and his family, who were indigent and came there for food and clothing. Theirs was an extremely tragic tale, long before this incident occurred.

As a result of this tragedy, I became very good friends with Sister Ruth, going there often to make donations. Every time I stopped by, she would tell me a story of one of the people who came to the shelter. One day she told me of a young woman who came with her two little girls, about five and six years old, asking if there were any shoes that would fit her daughters. Sister Ruth had only one pair, and gave it to the mother telling them she would go to the store and buy another pair of shoes. Each little girl took one shoe and put it on, and they were so excited to have one shoe. Just one shoe. That certainly gives you a different perspective on life.

For many, many years, I hosted huge Christmas parties at my home, and the purpose was that every guest was to bring an unwrapped, brand new toy for a child. A couple hundred people came to this annual party, allowing me to fill a van with gifts to take to Sister Ruth for the children there. When Sister Ruth retired at 77, I took 77 roses to her retirement party. We are not supposed to know why things happen the way they do, but looking back at this tragic event, as horrible as it is, it allowed me to play a major role in what was going on at the Day Star Center.

When I am speaking to audiences, my presentations are extemporaneous and designed for the specific audience, and while I have no shortage of real life stories, I don't always tell all of them. I did not talk about the accident at a presentation in Australia, but afterward, a woman came over to tell me, "Look, I've got to tell you something very strange. You were standing on the stage and there was a little boy standing next to you on your left hand side. It was really weird. I thought it was a reflection. I couldn't figure it out." I told her I knew what it probably was, and told her about the incident. This has happened more than once during my speaking events.

CHAPTER 8

BECAUSE OF MY SON

IT IS A TERRIBLE, HOLLOW FEELING TO BE 5,000 MILES AWAY FROM home when your son tells you that he's going to take his own life. I felt 100% helpless to do anything. The situation was so enormously painful that I don't actually recall the action I took, because I was in shock. It became strikingly clear my son just could not figure out life. I had hundreds of conversations with him over the years about why he was unable to find anything good in his life, and why he felt everything was painful.

He suffered from an inferiority complex that got so bad, at one point he walked around with a towel over his head. Many times he had been "Baker Acted" in Florida, which is when you become a danger to yourself or other people and the state takes over, placing him in a state-run, state-funded facility. When I would visit him, he would typically be drug induced to manage him, both emotionally and physically. He would be in a lockup with many people who all were in some state of sedation.

My observation was that the facility wasn't run with people who had extensive psychological skillsets. All I know is when he would leave there, he was not psychologically better. It became clear to me that he suffered from a combination of things that included an inferiority complex and very low self-worth. I'd been around him since he was two day old, and I was an attached parent. We weren't estranged, and it wasn't as if he lived in a different city. I could not fix my own disconnection from my father, and my father couldn't fix what had been handed down to me.

I had become my father, and my son had become me; an emotional dysfunction that wasn't consciously handed down. His life was a struggle. He had several jobs, and at one, he had to go to a conference and stand up and talk about himself. When he came home, he was in total shock as if he had a severe case of PTSD because he was asked to stand up in a room full of people. Shortly after, he was hospitalized again.

I tried everything I knew and everything I had learned. I read books and practiced skills with other people. It became clear to me that I was not able to help him because I had a vested emotional interest in him. Anything that I said was run through his own filter and it would come out as criticism in his mind. It wasn't meant that way. That's why I could work with other people's children and get huge successes, but I wasn't able to make progress with my son. I would send him to psychologists and he would come back and tell me that they were stupid and dysfunctional. At the time, I didn't have the in-depth skillset to recognize the traits of borderline personality disorder or BPD. Later, I learned the traits and currently work with many people whose children or significant others have BPD.

There is a book about borderline personality disorder called *I Hate You, Don't Leave Me*. It is very difficult to overcome that disorder. Many psychologists and psychiatrists do not like to take borderline patients because it is a tremendous amount of work, and not a high success rate. It is changeable, but it typically takes a long time.

There were numerous dynamics at play. First, it was passed down. I had my own father issues and we just swapped places. Second, he fit the borderline description. Trying to help him was an uphill battle, and when he reached puberty, it became evident this is what he was dealing with. Although I was not married to his mother, when he was young he was with me most of the time. In those early years, there wasn't anything wrong with him emotionally. We had constant interaction. I was not a distant dad. I was not a deadbeat dad in that I paid voluntary child support every week for 18 years, because that was the right thing to do.

Was I in his life as much as I needed to be to support his emotional health? No, not as I understand it now with my psychology skillset. At that time, I knew so many people who had children out of wedlock and simply walked away, never looking back. I did not do that. He was my biological son. I treated him the best way I knew how with the limited emotional skills I possessed. I didn't have a reference for being a nurturing father.

I gave his eulogy to a packed house. If there is one thing that should never happen to a parent, it would be to bury your child. My grandmother had to do it, and she was never the same person again. The pain is so excruciating, it is difficult to put into words. His mother visits his gravesite regularly, but I will never visit his gravesite. I cannot look at my son's name on a gravestone with a beginning date and an ending date with a dash in between.

One day, I was sitting in the parking lot of Home Depot thinking about the pain and suffering we had both gone through. I grow from my life's painful experiences. I said a little prayer. I said "Jay, will you please forgive me for not being who you wanted and needed me to be? I am sorry, will you forgive me?" I sat in the car and said that several times. The next night, Jason came to me in a dream. He was standing in a boat and I was talking to him. I was thinking to myself in the dream, "Thank God I caught him, and can talk to him before he does what he did. Thank God I caught him." Through his life, every time I saw Jason we would hug, but my hug was a real hug and his was frozen. During this dream, it was the first time his hug had emotion, love, and compassion. His hug was long, and it represented a whole life of missed hugs. It was so overwhelming, all I could do was cry. I couldn't say anything to him. It was as if our hug was saved up for 30 years of his 40-year life. The dream was vivid, lucid and extremely powerful.

Life is not what we think it is. We wander around looking for love instead of giving love. He heard my prayer. He came to me in a dream and said, "Dad, it's okay. I'm okay. You're okay. We're okay." You can't make this up. I have a sense he's my angel, and he is going to do the best for me from the other side so that I can do the best for other people on this side. That is his gift to me and is one I will pass on. My legacy in the name of my son is to help as many people as I can worldwide who not only suffer from Bi-Polar Disorder, but those who just suffer like returning military who have such a limited amount of resources it makes me sad to just think about it.

CHAPTER 9

A LIFETIME OF SUPPRESSION

AFTER A LONG DAY OF WORK, A FRIEND WAS MASSAGING MY FEET WHEN I started having pain in my knee. Within five minutes, I was lying on the floor in a fetal position having convulsions. Ten hours later, I was in the hospital where I was in critical condition.

My left leg had grown to three times its normal size all the way to my hip, and the doctors misdiagnosed me as having a massive strep infection. My white blood count was out of control, and I had massive amounts of anti-biotics, but my condition continued to worsen and I fell unconscious.

I was released from the hospital two weeks later, having no muscle mass in my left leg. It was like the leg of a rag doll, and I couldn't do anything with it at all. I couldn't move it, I couldn't use it. I couldn't walk. I was misdiagnosed again. It wasn't a strep infection after all.

I went to numerous doctors to figure out what had happened to me, and was finally diagnosed by Chinese sports medicine doctor, Dr. Hogan Yi. RSD stands for Reflex Sympathetic Dystrophy. Reflex: Reaction. Sympathetic: Nervous System. Dystrophy: Deterioration.

RSD is an autoimmune disease where your nervous system responds and the responses are counterintuitive, or the opposite of what is expected.

You have two immune systems: A physical immune system and an emotional one. A simplified way of explaining what RSD is: You're walking down a hallway, and I'm walking towards you carrying a fork in my hand when I accidentally bump your arm with the fork. It doesn't break your skin, but you react as if it did. Reflex: Reaction. Your reflex is "Ouch!" but your nervous system provides the wrong command and says, "Oh. Pain. You want pain." So, your nervous system manufactures the pain. Your body's reflex to pain is to give you more. It is my experience that this is what can happen when you've spent your entire life suppressing emotion. Unfortunately, there is no treatment for RSD, no cure, and they have not yet come to a medical reason why people get it.

Since I'd lost all the muscle mass in my leg, I had to go to therapy every day to learn to walk again. It wasn't going well, as nothing was improving. Each day I would go and lie on a mat and try to lift my leg, but I couldn't move it.

The physical therapy department was in a huge common area on the top floor of a hospital and at any given time, dozens of people were in the process of trying to learn to walk again. I was on a floor with all of these people, young and old, who had a physical trauma they were working to overcome. Every day my physical therapist told me to lift my leg off the mat, and every day I couldn't. This went on for weeks, and I grew increasingly frustrated. Why wasn't this working?

I began manufacturing thoughts like, "I'll never be able to snow ski again. I'll never be able to roller skate again. I'll never be able to do physical labor. I'll never be able to climb stairs." I thought my life as I knew it was ruined.

One of my friends who had lost the use of both legs in an accident was also there in therapy. I watched him on the hand bars and thought to myself, "I wonder how much of all this is mental, and how much is physical?" That day I left the hospital wondering what would happen if I hypnotize myself in an effort to heal my leg.

I laid on my bed and put myself in a trance, giving myself an embedded command, a message of powerful suggestion to my subconscious mind. Putting yourself in a trance simply means you have narrowed your focus to one single point, disregarding everything else. Some might call it meditation. I meditated. I made my only thought the movement of my leg. Prior to this exercise, my only thought was the non-movement of my left. For at least 30 minutes, I put every single bit of my consciousness into the movement of my leg.

I focused and visualized raising my leg three feet off the bed and said aloud, "Okay, lift your leg." I lifted my leg two feet off the bed.

The next morning I went to therapy and shocked the therapist. She couldn't understand how I could make so much progress overnight. What shook her up more was when I told her that after coming here all these weeks and watching these people, it seemed the emotional aspect of healing is more powerful than the physical aspect.

I enjoyed extreme activities. I was a snow skier, a roller skater, I've raced motorcycles, and more. Going through injury, then allowing your imagination to focus on never being the same again brings up a lot of emotion, compounding things.

I watched the expressions of those people in the common area, and knew some of the personally. You could see their imagination was going crazy, and it had nothing to do with them healing. It was actually causing the opposite to happen. In physical therapy, I've wondered what percentage of the healing process is physical, and what is emotional? There should also be emotional therapy to go along with physical therapy.

I certainly can't say that about all physical therapists across the world, but I can say it about my experience. I can tell you for sure that if there were an emotional component to physical therapy it would change the healing time.

Doctors know the human mind plays an enormous role in how the body functions, so much so that they can give sugar pills (placebos) to people who don't know it and cure sickness and disease.

When you attach your emotions to your imagination, it can be the greatest gift because you can create miracles that way.

When you have an operating system inside your subconscious created by a foundation of pain based on childhood experiences, you are unconsciously matching up what goes on inside of you to your outside circumstances. You are unconsciously choosing people and experiences that fulfill and match up to the operating system. It is counterintuitive.

If you are managing the effects of the original cause, and the original cause is low self-worth, the original cause has its basis in painful experiences that you equate to:

I'm unlovable

I'm unloved

I'm disliked

I'm at fault

I'm not enough

People often attempt to use their physical body to overcome an emotional hurdle, and it is counterintuitive. It is backward. Your emotions start giving you messages that aren't healthy, and you are focusing on them, thereby hypnotizing yourself into a state of not being healed and not being functional.

Four days before my 50th birthday, I accidentally discovered that my long time best friend, Johnny Green, had spent almost a year arranging a huge surprise birthday party for me. The week before, I noticed a very strange sensation right over my heart; it was a slight buzz or something like an electrical shock. When I looked in the mirror at my chest, I noticed a very small black dot, like what a pencil would make, it was barely noticeable. I have a very dear friend, Dr. Richard Phares, who was a local plastic surgeon, so I went to his office; to have him look at the spot. He decided to take a biopsy, and within two days, he called to tell me he had scheduled surgery for me Friday morning: the day of my birthday, and the night of the surprise party. I advised him to change the surgery to Monday, to which he replied, "You don't understand. You have a malignant melanoma right over your heart. You can't wait until Monday."

I have always had an interesting belief about the human body and the power to heal itself. I had also had a history of refusing surgeries: radical knee surgery, both torn rotator cuffs, and losing the use of one of my fingers, all of which I was able to recover fully from without surgery. My body healed itself. So in this too, I declined the cancer surgery.

Dr. Phares was beside himself saying, "Are you crazy? Come to my office Friday morning, when the office is closed. I will give you a local anesthetic and cut your chest open to remove it." I was given a gift on my 50th birthday; Dr. Richard Phares saved my precious life. In my world, he is a man with a huge heart, a kind soul, and an angel in a human body. I left his office with a bandage covering a huge chest incision from my neckline to my waist. I kept the whole situation a secret from my family and friends, including wearing a T-shirt when swimming to cover the scar. I never returned for a follow up. One has to have a certain kind of emotional immune system to support that kind of decision. I tell people, "Don't try this at home." Just because I did this and was successful at it, I am not telling you to try this. I learned something about my physical body in a way that other people don't typically understand.

This whole situation poses an interesting hypothesis. Why was the malignant melanoma directly over my heart? The same heart that, by my own life choices had been broken so many times I had lost count. I had suffered through the life experiences that hurt in the "matters of the heart". It is no medical secret that stress causes disease. My belief is that the years of dysfunctional relationships and friendships had continuously broken my heart. It was my choice to stay connected to the toxic relationships; it was not my choice to compromise my immune system to the point of a life threatening disease. The stress verses optimum health is an interesting hypothesis. How does it apply to things like breast cancer, organ cancer, infant cancer, or even animal cancer? It poses the question: Is there a major emotional factor that seriously affects our physical health that we as humans are not conscious of with regard to our physical body? Again, consider the possibility that the human body may in fact have two distinct and separate immune systems: emotional and physical. The emotional manages the physical.

Do we put too much faith in what authority figures have to say? Do we overlook our own gift of healing based on the miracle of the human body and all its abilities? Do we contemplate the placebo effect and only half way except it as fact? Do we short-circuit our own body's ability to heal, based on the stress we are willing to accept and maintain in the name of a destination somewhere off in the future? Do we compromise living in the now, by looking back at all the things we should have done or could have done? Do we push our way through life with questionable self-worth, the hidden source of unimaginable stress? In the last 30 months, I have lost 19 of my long-time friends, 13 to disease, and 6 to taking their own precious lives. What part did ongoing stress play in the loss of their lives? In many cases, allowing your heart to be broken is a choice that comes from a place deep inside the subconscious, where low self-worth is the ultimate decision maker.

CHAPTER 10

I WOULD TRADE EVERYTHING FOR INNER PEACE.

THERE IS A GROWING PROBLEM CALLED THE SPONTANEOUS SUICIDE. One may not necessarily walk around contemplating ending their life, but then a series of things happen without their having a quality emotional support system.

I had periods where I didn't have the courage to end the pain, and I didn't have the courage to live it either. The courage to live it meaning to experience what there is to experience, and feel it.

In order to heal it, you must feel it.

Do not attach your imagination to those emotions in a way that you are creating additional trauma to yourself. If healing those emotions requires therapy, you should obtain professional help.

Once when I was financially broke, my doorbell rang and a long-time friend told me she was in real trouble. She was going to lose her real estate office and needed to borrow $2,000. All I had to my name was $600 in the bank, but I gave it to her. Later, it came to my attention she had spent the $600 on drugs.

Several years later, I received a letter from her attorney telling me she had claimed personal bankruptcy and consequently I would not be receiving the $600 owed to me. I thought about what a slimy move that is. I would have been okay if I'd received a note from her that said, "Gary, I borrowed $600 from you, and if it takes me my whole lifetime, I will pay you back, $5.00 at a time." But to get a letter from an attorney saying she'd claimed personal bankruptcy? I would say that person is ethically, morally and spiritually bankrupt. The financial bankruptcy is the least of the issue.

At that time, I owned my business and my home free and clear, had minimal debt and had many material assets. I journaled often and I remember writing:

I would trade everything I own for inner peace.

What a bold statement. I would have traded everything I personally owned for peace of mind. That's where the wisdom is. I didn't have peace of mind because I was doing what everyone else was doing. If you want a different result, don't do what everyone else does. Lying will never give you peace of mind. Not forgiving yourself and other people will never give you peace of mind. I had never forgiven myself for many things, like the accident and cheating on my wife. I didn't know anything about the traits of self-worth. I never learned them. I never had the option. They were not written on a chalkboard in school.

If you want to have no inner peace, then lie and justify the lies. Do not forgive yourself and other people.

If you want to have inner peace, understand that peace is a byproduct of self-worth. This doesn't mean you will never experience loss, grief, being lied to, being used, betrayal, or abuse. It just means that when you experience those things, you will experience them in a completely different way, and you will not allow those events to steal your inner peace.

When I was 30, I built my home with a friend, Gary Lieberman. At the time, it was the largest house on the island, but having this distinction did not give me inner peace. What it gave me was a much bigger tax bill and larger maintenance bills. It had to be fed. It didn't feed me. It wasn't an asset; it was a liability. It's only an asset when you deposit the home's worth in a bank account.

I did all the wrong things in attempting to find inner peace. I now understand that life is not about having inner peace 24/7. If I had that notebook sitting on my bed stand now, I would write:

There's no one I would rather be than me.

CHAPTER 11

NEVER HAVE A RELATIONSHIP WITH SOMEONE'S POTENTIAL

AFTER THE 27-YEAR RELATIONSHIP WITH THE WOMAN ENDED, IT WAS time that I took a deep look inside of myself to find out what caused me to keep letting her back into my life. Through ongoing therapy with three different therapists, I learned that I had become what's termed as "object constancy" to her. In other words, she knew I would always be there to rescue her and used that to her advantage. In fairness, I subconsciously enabled her.

I also needed to figure out what caused me to accept this sort of behavior that caused me great pain. I was diagnosed with "euphoric recall", where I was incapable of recognizing the damaging and dysfunctional aspects of the relationship, only the euphoric moments. I could not see that she lacked self-worth and authenticity, and that she was dishonest and emotionally unavailable. I didn't have a problem identifying those traits in other romantic relationships I'd had, only with her.

She did teach me the importance of emotional availability, trust and self-worth because she lacked all of them. Her behavior was her behavior, and I played a part in it. In retrospect, she gave me the gift of awareness. In accelerating her dysfunction, my growth was accelerated because it gave me the courage to look inside myself and find healing.

In her astounding book, *The Sociopath Next Door*, Martha Stout, Ph.D. says, "*Imagine - if you can - not having a conscience, none at all, no feelings of guilt or remorse no matter what you do, no limiting sense of concern for the well-being of strangers, friends, or even family members. Imagine no struggles with shame, not a single one in your life, no matter what kind of selfish, lazy harmful or immoral action you have taken.*" Yes, 4% of the population of the United States alone goes through life with zero conscience.

You must create an ability to look inside yourself, and understand the people on your relationship path are all bringing something with them, that is, their childhood experiences. Whatever hasn't been resolved from childhood will be magnified in an intimate relationship with another person. The tendency is to go to any extreme to hide what they are ashamed of and have never dealt with. If you want a successful intimate relationship, you must have trust. You must feel safe and be able to communicate emotionally on any level without the risk of feeling wrong. If your feelings are questioned and you don't feel comfortable sharing them, then you're in an unhealthy relationship, which will never work.

When you try to manipulate the outside world, it never works because you cannot control what goes on outside you. The gift of human life is to realize that the outside world is a reflection of the inside world.

Never have a relationship with someone's potential.

Do not attempt a relationship with their potential to be somebody different than they are right in the moment that you are with them.

Avoid seeing the person for who they are **not**. Failure to do that that causes people to stay in relationships for extended periods and the relationship becomes more dysfunctional. It also becomes much harder to get out of when you do that.

You may be curious as to why I would choose someone who did not have the capacity to like or love me. I could not get her to like me or love me, so I determined that I must not be likable or lovable. In a complex way, I was proving myself right. This emotional foundation was deep in my subconscious, and I realized it was my subconscious mind that chose the woman, not my conscious mind.

Through therapy, I was guided to understand the woman was a strong representation of my Father and my need to heal the past. As a result, I was finally free of the chains that held me from complete emotional freedom.

In creating a life well lived, we must consider the factors that actually provide our desired result. Love relationships play such a significant part of human life with regard to getting our emotional, physical, financial, and in many cases, parenting needs met. I would consider it critical to have a basic understanding of the most common personality and character disorders to help guide you through a maze of relationship choices.

Sometimes those who seem trustworthy or charming are seductive manipulators who can charm you right out of your precious life. To know the traits of narcissistic, borderline, sociopathic and chronic co-dependent behavior gives you an enormous advantage when choosing a life partner. Further, understanding your own underlying emotional voids helps you make healthy authentic decisions.

Choose wisely, not based on physical, compatibility, or financial factors. Instead, your choices should be based on character and virtue. Then you have a much better chance of having a relationship well lived.

Remember, the outside world is a giant reflection of your internal world.

CHAPTER 12

I HAVE TO BE WHAT I'M SEARCHING FOR

WHEN I WAS HAVING RELATIONSHIPS ISSUES, I WENT TO A RELATIONSHIP coach and therapist and told him of the woman I was in a 27 year relationship with. It took an hour and ten minutes to relay all that occurred. When I was through, he said, "Let me ask you a question. In order of importance, what are five qualities you look for in a person?" I fired off this list:

1. Honest
2. Emotionally Available
3. Healthy Self-worth
4. Spiritual
5. Emotionally Balanced

His was response to me was, "Wow, that's a great list! Why did you choose a person who didn't have <u>any</u> of those qualities?"

Then he had me consider an opportunity where I would be able to choose a woman who had all the qualities I sought, saying I was (metaphorically) going to interview 100 women, asking them anything, and for as long as I wanted. In this exercise, physical attraction was not going to be an issue because I would be physically attracted to all, but only ten of the 100 women will have the qualities I seek.

He asked me, "How will you know which are the ten women out of the 100?" I was pondering his question when he threw a curve ball and told me, "What you don't know is that all 100 women have studied your character profile, knowing your strengths, weaknesses, and history. They know more about you than YOU know about you. Now, how will you determine which ten women meet your criteria?"

The appointment ended. He never told me the answer of how I would choose, but I figured it out. If you keep making choices that are self-destructive, what has to change for you to make better decisions on your relationship choices? Have you identified what character traits you absolutely need in a relationship? How will you know if someone meets those needs, if you haven't identified them first?

Having read 2,200 books and spending 25 years involved in the personal development industry, you begin to look at life in a different way. One of the first things you must come to know is:

I have to be what I am looking for.

Once you have become what you are looking for, it gives you the ability to see what you can't see when you're looking for people who have qualities that you don't have. When YOU possess the qualities you seek, you can easily see them in others, and you can recognize those who don't have them. If you are looking for someone who possesses the wonderful qualities of being emotionally available, emotionally balanced, honest with a healthy self-worth, but those qualities are not present in you, the relationship just isn't going to work.

CHAPTER 13

WHAT'S NOT ON YOUR LIST?

IN MANY OF MY PRESENTATIONS, I WILL DO AN EXERCISE WITH THE audience that we are going to do here. I will hand out 3 x 5 index cards to everyone in the audience and ask them to write the numbers 1 through 5 on the left side of the card.

TIME TO TAKE ACTION

Write down the five qualities you look for in a person that you want to be in a relationship with in order of importance. You have 60 seconds. GO!

There are no right or wrong answers to this exercise. Before reading further, make sure you have written your list.

When I do this exercise on stage, it is absolutely amazing to watch what is going on with the audience, half of them staring at the ceiling as if the answers could be found there. When the 60 seconds have passed, I invite people to share their list and some very interesting answers are revealed, like:

» Tall

» Financially secure

» Likes to snow ski

» Likes to travel

» Sense of humor

Every once in a while, there is something of real substance shared. Since there isn't time for everyone to read their cards, I tell them we're going to do some research and ask:

"Raise your hand if you wrote healthy self-worth." No one raises their hand.

"Raise your hand if you wrote emotionally available." Again, no one raises their hand, but there are usually murmurs of people saying "Hmmm... I didn't think to write that down."

"Raise your hand if you wrote honest." One person raises their hand.

"Now ladies, can you have a relationship with a man who is not emotionally available?", and the woman yell out, "No!"

I tell them, "You know you can't have a relationship with a man who is not emotionally available, but you didn't write it down on your list?"

What did YOU write on your list?

A few years ago, I was sitting in a restaurant with a friend, when another walked in and joined us. She had been married 26 years and was going through a painful divorce, her heart was broken because her husband had an affair.

I grabbed a napkin and asked her to write numbers 1 through 5 on it, then asked her, "Write down the top five qualities you looked for in this man you married." When I asked what she'd written as the first one, she said she noticed he was wearing very expensive alligator shoes. The second item on the list was 'financially secure'. I don't remember the other three she listed. It isn't important. What IS important is that she didn't write "honesty", a trait she clearly thought was valuable to her.

What is not on your list that should be?

Chapter 14

PTSD

PTSD, meaning Post Traumatic Stress Disorder is commonly associated with the military. Prior to its use, it was commonly referred to as "shell shock" from the trauma soldiers experienced during horrific acts of warfare. It is now a mainstream term for those outside the military who have witnessed or experienced horrific acts.

It can occur after traumatic events like experiencing or witnessing violent personal attacks, car accidents, rape, physical, emotional or sexual abuse, losing a child, to mention just a few.

The Veteran statistics are horrifying with one in three returning troops being diagnosed with serious PTSD symptoms[1]. How many civilians have PTSD? The number is staggering. An estimated 8% of Americans or 24.4 million people will experience PTSD at some point in their lives[1].

I developed PTSD as a result of being traumatized when I was a child and have lived with it most of my life, recurring more frequently in the last three years.

There are different degrees of PTSD because in most cases it creates disorder in your life. The disorder creates behaviors that range from agitation, irritability, hostility, and self-destructive behavior to social isolation. The psychological effects include flashback fear, severe anxiety or mistrust. The often hidden effects of PTSD are guilt, loneliness or an inability to feel pleasure. Symptoms that are more common are insomnia, nightmares, emotional detachment or unwanted thoughts. Often you lack emotional order and are unable to find peace within yourself, unable to process the emotions you feel.

Perhaps, if we learned emotional well-being and how to manage our emotions early in life, we would be less likely to experience PTSD. Most people do not know how to process their emotions.

PTSD can be easily triggered. Proper treatment for PTSD includes recognizing the nature of situations that inflame it. For example, military PTSD victims should likely stay away from fireworks displays. Personally, I could not go into my home office for years, as my son had worked there with me. I had to move out of my own home to avoid seeing the three people that were staying there against my will. My insomnia is ongoing and intermittent self-isolation occurs.

I was teetering on a PTSD attack when a close friend of 40 years said some things that triggered an attack that sent me into self-isolation for two days. He didn't know he did it.

After not seeing my friend in a few years, I received an email from him telling me he had seen me at a store, and wanted to come up and give me a hug, but didn't because he couldn't understand how I could travel all over the world preaching forgiveness, and not forgive him.

I can tell you, had I seen him at Sam's Club I would have instantly run up and gave him a hug. I wouldn't have even thought twice about it. He saw me and made a determination that he had done something that I needed to forgive him for, when the reality is that the comment he made had no negative intention behind it.

When I started having more frequent episodes, I wanted my friends to know how to avoid my PTSD triggers. There is a lot of information online and a great resource is a book called *Getting Past The Past* by Francine Shapiro.

When I read the email from my friend, I wrote back. "I have nothing to forgive you for. My brain processes your comments as a judgment calling me a hypocrite. This is the very reason that I have to be careful and conscious of my surroundings." That is the reason I disconnected. That's the very thing I avoid because it's not in my best interest to do that. He never responded. Odds are he doesn't know how.

I've lost some friendships because some do not know how PTSD works and how to avoid triggering it.

When you get to the stage when the PTSD is overwhelming, unless you are reaching out to people who are psychologists, you have to be careful. PTSD can be triggered by people who only want to love you, hug you, and help you. The problem is they don't know how to do it because they have never had the personal experience of the PTSD. Once you've had that, you know what to say and what not to say.

Chapter 15

A FEW UPSIDES

To be sure, my life is not comprised of only strikeouts. I had some real home runs sprinkled in. In the early 80s, I would periodically meet with an artist friend of mine, Betsy Schott. We would go to a bookstore and buy a half a dozen travel magazines and colorful poster boards. We sat on my living room floor and chose places we wanted to visit, and things that we wanted to appear in our lives. It was a fun ritual process. People now call it treasure mapping or vision boarding.

One day, I cut out a photograph of Tony Robbins, taken when he was around 20 years old. He was wearing a suit and tie, shoes off and his pant legs were rolled-up as he walked across hot coals. I pasted that photograph on the poster board. The next photograph I cut out was a full-page ad in a travel magazine for a Hilton Hotel in Honolulu, Hawaii, because Hawaii was one of my dream places to visit. The idea of this exercise is that you are to periodically take these images and stare at them, never questioning whether it will happen or not. You were just to accept that whatever you placed on that board was reality. I've done many of these boards and it is an extremely powerful example of the law of attraction.

For a few months, we were both very excited about periodically looking at these posters, and then eventually they all wound up in a stack under the bed in my guest room, staying there for years.

Between the time I'd made those posters and when I finally looked at them again, I had become a professional artist, as a professional sand sculptor. I travelled all over the world creating enormous sand castle projects. When I say "enormous", I mean Enormous. My creations ranged from 18 to 55 feet in height.

One day I was looking for something and happened along the stack of long forgotten posters. I looked at the one with the Hilton ad again. At the time I pasted the photo, I hadn't noticed the ad showed the Hilton Hotel, but the photograph was taken from a long way off. There was an inlet bay between the hotel and photographer.

Because at the time I was manifesting Hawaii when I cut out the photograph, I didn't notice that in the foreground was a sandy beach. In that foreground, between the cameraman and the inlet, was a little boy and girl leaning down, carving on a sand castle, with an older gentleman standing next to them.

I looked at the vision board, puzzled thinking, "There's just no way that image could have manifested a 14-year professional artist career, because I never even noticed it. Or could it?" It wasn't as if I saw the sand castle, and decided to manifest that. At the time, I didn't even see the sand castle. My field of vision had to do with the Hilton hotel and going to Hawaii.

The man who taught me the art of sand sculpting is the most well-known sand sculptor on earth named Gerry Kirk. Under another manifestation story, he and I became partners and travelled all over the world.

I called Gerry up and said, "Gerry, you won't even believe this, but I'm looking at a manifestation poster. I happened to notice that there's a sand castle in the foreground that I never noticed before." Gerry began laughing, and I said, "Yeah, it's for a Hilton ad I did years ago."

Wow! Did I manifest a career out of something that I wasn't even trying to manifest, simply because my mind saw what my physical eye didn't see?

Fast forward a few years and I wound up working with Tony Robbins. At the time and for ten years following, Tony's major event was in Hawaii each year. Every year I spent three weeks in a five-star hotel in Hawaii. I actually manifested what I set out to do, which was going to Hawaii. However, I didn't just manifest going there. I manifested spending three weeks a year there in a five-star hotel.

Later, as Director of Security, I was invited, along with two men on my team, to go to Tony's resort in Fiji for an eight-day vacation. There are two routes to get to the international airport of Nadi, Los Angeles direct to Nadi, or Los Angeles to Honolulu to Nadi. On the return flight, we had to overnight in Honolulu.

When I originally pulled the photo of the hotel in Hawaii, I did not know it was the Hilton in Honolulu with a 20-story mosaic rainbow. The morning of our outgoing flight, we took a long walk, and when we got to the end of the sidewalk bordering the beach, I noticed there were thousands of pieces of tile on the side of the building. I looked up and realized I was at the foot of that mosaic rainbow!

I reached in my pocket, grabbed my cell phone, and called my friend Betsy saying, "Betsy, you're not going to believe this but I'm standing at the foot of the rainbow from the page that I tore out of the travel magazine. I'm actually standing at the foot of that rainbow!"

I have at least fifty experiences like this that are absolutely profound to me. It all has to do with the fact that we are all connected in ways we don't often realize.

Often I traveled the world doing sand sculpture projects for the Japanese and Holland governments. I was an invited guest at the International Performing Arts Festival in Singapore, which happens twice a year. Every other year artists are invited from all over the world to perform at the festival. Our performance was sand sculpting as a performing art. It was there that my work captured the attention of someone who got in touch with me to request I create a sand sculpture replica of the White House for President Clinton, who was planning a visit to Treasure Island.

I wanted it to be architecturally accurate and scaled correctly, but the problem was that President Clinton is tall, and for it to impact and impress him, it needed to be as tall or taller than he was. If I made the White House as tall as him, it would be a half a city block long in scale. For security reasons, the secret service wouldn't give me access to some details I needed to recreate the White House in sand.

Finally, I decided to do the Presidential Seal because the Seal is on everything having to do with the President. Although the Secret Service knew it would take four days to build the Presidential Seal replica, they still had not given me permission to begin. At 6:00 the night before it had to be finished by 7:00 a.m., I was on the way to a Chamber of Commerce mixer and remembered something I had heard about shaping my future. I knew I had to make a decision.

I called Susan, the Director of Tourism for St. Petersburg and the event President Clinton was attending, and asked her what the status was on creating the sand sculpture. She called the head of the Secret Service and said, "I have Mr. King sitting in front of me, and he wants to know if he can do this or not?" I knew it would take me four days to do it, and I sat there thinking, "What a mess this is going to be if they say 'yes' this late in the game!" Suddenly she said, "Okay thank you. They said you could do it. Go."

I jumped in my car and I called my friends, my son, called everybody I could get telling them, "I'm in trouble. I have to do this project, and it requires a bobcat and tools, and so many other things. We have until 7:00 in the morning to finish this." I asked all these people for buckets and all this stuff, went down there and started.

By midnight, I had a couple of failures; things weren't working out, pieces broke off. I was freaking out. By 5:00AM, there were around 10,000 people there on the beach. I finished it. President Clinton was supposed to come at 7:00AM.

People were waiting, and the crowd was building to around 15,000 people. The White House Press Corp was there, as well as every imaginable news media. The whole area was roped off, and I was exhausted, lying on a lounger 200 feet away in shorts and a T-shirt.

The Secret Service was all over the place. There were helicopters in the air and riflemen on the roof of the hotel. Suddenly the Secret Service announced, "President Clinton has already left for the day; he will not be coming out onto the beach. His schedule changed, and he's already gone."

About a third of the people left so I figured the Secret Service was thinning the crowd. I waited another half an hour, and sure enough, President Clinton came out. He walked up into the quarantined off area, and I heard him yell something like "Oh my God who did this? Who did this?" One of the Secret Service men found me and took me over to the President. He was hugging me with one arm, and asking me questions. The next morning was an enormous full-color picture of the President hugging me and pointing at the sand sculpture on the front page of the paper.

I didn't ever think I would be on the front page of the newspaper with the President of the United States, but the United Press International picked up on it. It was on the front page of every newspaper in the United States. My friend, Gerry Kirk from San Diego called me saying, "G, you are on the front page of the San Diego paper! I have been sand sculpting my whole life, and I have never been on the front page of the paper with the President of the United States." I said, "Well Gary, it's like this: I'm on the front page of the newspaper with the President because of you. If I had never crossed paths with you, this wouldn't have happened."

As a result, Disney called me. They were in the process of building a new ride, and hired me to do a sand sculpture on the beach in the middle of the night so that no one would know. They flew a film crew in at sunrise to film it for a commercial.

Yes indeed. I have had amazing home runs. How many people wind up on the front page of the newspaper with the President of the United States? Here is another fun part of that story. I took the picture, had it professionally enlarged and framed at 2 feet by 3 feet, signed it and shipped it to the White House. At the time, I wondered what would happen to it. When I returned from a trip, there was a message waiting for me: "This is President Clinton's office. Would you please give us a call?" Because so many people knew what I'd done, I thought someone was pulling a joke on me, but I called the number, and a woman answered the phone "President Clinton's office. Oh Mr. King, we have been trying to reach you. President Clinton has a gift for you and we need an address." What did I get? I got a 2 x 3 foot autographed, professionally framed picture of the President and me. He had autographed the picture and wrote, "Thank you for the great work." It hangs on my office wall.

CHAPTER 16

THERE'S NOTHING MORE IMPORTANT THAN YOUR CHARACTER

CORPORATE FRAUD APPEARS TO BE COMPLETELY OUT OF CONTROL worldwide. It is as if we have turned "Free Enterprise" into a free for all foundation of lying, cheating, marketing deception, emotional manipulation and emotional abuse, all in the name of money, profit and power.

In the classic case of the "Fall of Enron" the worldwide energy company, founder Kenneth Lay was convicted of ten counts of corporate fraud and conspiracy, and while awaiting sentencing, he unexpectedly dropped dead of a massive heart attack. Could it be possible that after hearing weeks of testimony about his underhanded, unscrupulous, greedy practices, he just simply "broke his own heart", the emotional overwhelm just too much for a human heart to withstand?

This also speaks to the ongoing practice of humans who are so driven to succeed in the creation of massive wealth, power and arrogance, that they are forced to "switch off their conscience" in order to operate with no ethical and moral foundation. The lesson to this behavior: NEVER switch off your conscience. It could cost you your family, your friendships, your marriage, your character, and ultimately your precious life, all in the name of controlling the external world, rather than the internal world. There is NO external substitute for inner peace, physical health and well-being and your right to Happiness.

There is nothing more important than your character.

There are more than 1,280,000 hits on my quote. If there is nothing more important than your character, then that is a predetermined foundation. You do not have to make a decision at the moment based on potential consequences or the potential upside. You don't have to decide whether you're going to get caught or going to make more money or lose money. You don't have to think about those things because your character is most important. If you violate your character, you are not working towards your greatest benefit to the law of cause and effect, and the law of compounding. You deceive yourself into thinking you can somehow cheat the system and win.

That doesn't work, because even if you can cheat the external system, your internal system won't be cheated. We all have a conscience, and even if that conscience were masked over, it still exists. Call it the spirit, the soul, or whatever, but it exists.

CHAPTER 17

YOU HAVE BEEN INFLUENCED

THE AMOUNT OF TIME SPENT IN DISTRACTION, WATCHING TELEVISION or on the internet averages more than 20 hours per week per person. Much of the content on TV is mindless, often violent or sexual, and most of it advertises negativity with no social value. Only 10% of it has what I would call quality emotional value. I watch the History Channel, American Greed and later on in the evening, the news. The only reason I watch the news is because in my presentations and on the internet, Facebook and email, I'm often asked my opinion about certain domestic or international scenarios, so I watch to stay current in order to give intelligent, factual feedback or opinion.

Other than that, I watch documentaries. I will watch the program American Greed, about the abuse of power and money. I don't watch it as entertainment; I'm studying the human behavior.

I go to the shopping malls, and I see a fascinating thing I call obligation marketing. You're walking through the mall, and there's a kiosk with six people cleaning eyeglasses. They call you over, telling you they want to clean your glasses for you, and they don't want to sell you anything. As soon as they clean your glasses, you feel obligated to buy the cleaner because they've given you something you didn't earn. Obligation marketing.

In movie theaters, there are subliminal marketing ploys you'd never notice. You see an eye catching liquor advertisement graphic in a magazine with a beautiful woman holding an empty glass with ice cubes and a bottle of liquor. Does anything look different or odd about it? Focus on the ice cubes. There's no liquid, but look closely at the cracks in the ice. They spell s-e-x. When you look at it again, you wonder how you missed it. You miss it all the time.

Somebody influenced you that it is not appropriate to forgive someone if you have been raped, beaten, been stolen from or cheated on. You have been influenced that the appropriate response to these actions are to get even. That's how you've been influenced. How are you influencing others?

Are you influencing them to benefit yourself or are you influencing them to benefit themselves? When I say to an audience of women, "Be clear, there is no such thing as an unattractive woman. There are only women who think those thoughts." There are only standards that we create. Frankly if you were the only woman on planet earth, you'd have no reference. You would have nobody to compare yourself to so you would be clueless. What's the result of that kind of belief system?

Women tend to rank themselves based on their perception of their looks. Based on how you have been influenced, if you are a teenage girl and you have ranked your looks as a four, will you ever change from a four to a nine? Not likely unless you learn why you chose the four to begin with, then you can change it. You made a choice to rank yourself a four, and you made that choice because somebody was either consciously or subconsciously influencing you about who you are, what your limitations are, and your physical presence. You are being influenced either to sell you something to take advantage of you or in some way to conquer you.

If you were never taught about this and never made aware, then it's going to happen constantly to you. It will lead you down a path where someday you wake up saying, "My life is a mess". Yes, because that is your primary thought process, my life is a mess.

It is never your circumstances that define your future. It is your choices.

If you have experienced traumatic circumstances and you choose to suppress them, you will do yourself emotional damage. Most people believe that external circumstances cause inner turmoil, but the reality is what you're dealing with internally creates your external world.

I researched what centenarians, people older than 100, have in common. There are many things, but these seven appear to be the most common in the United States.

1. They all worked for a living. One woman in particular, was 112 years old and at the time, she was a tour guide in a mansion outside of Atlanta.
2. They all have a positive mental attitude.
3. They all believe in something larger than themselves, so they had a spiritual foundation.
4. They ate what they loved and loved what they ate.
5. They had resolved any issues associated with loss.
6. They were all conscious of the benefits of reading and constantly expanding their mental capacity.
7. Strength of character: A virtuous life is directly connected to physical well-being.

The work of positive psychologists like Martin Seligman appears to show that the happiest people are those that have discovered their unique strengths (such as persistence and critical thinking) and virtues (such as humanity or justice) and use those strengths and virtues for a purpose that is greater than their own personal goals.

Chapter 18

THE LAW OF COMPOUNDING

MOST PEOPLE CONSIDER THE LAW OF COMPOUNDING HAS SOMETHING to do with the financial world. You rarely hear the term "compounding" connected to behavior.

In my presentations, I say to audiences, "I'm giving you a choice: I will give you $50,000 in cash right now, or I will give you a penny doubled for 30 days. Which will you choose?" Most people raise their hand and want the $50,000.

A few will ask for the penny doubled. When I ask them, "Why? How much is it?" they usually answer, "I don't know. It's just a lot." They do not know. I tell them, "A penny doubled for 30 days is $5,368,709.12." As you can imagine, that shocks them. If you take it to 35 days, it is now $160 million. Google "a penny doubled" and it will show you the chart. It is difficult to imagine because your brain is doing this: Two cents, four cents, eight cents, sixteen, 32, 64, 128, 254...there's no way. There's no possible way you can turn $2.54 into $5 million. Yes, there is. It is the Law of Compounding.

Everything in life compounds. The Law of Compounding applies to human emotions and behavior. It is directly connected. Once you start practicing The Happiness Formula®, it is bound and controlled by the Law of Compounding. If you practice just one of the three elements, it will compound rapidly.

If you research the penny-doubled example, you will find that the most profound compounding effect that takes it from two cents to $5 million dollars happens in the last five days. I applied that same law to the Happiness Formula®. The farther you go forward, the more it exponentially increases.

CHAPTER 19

CAUGHT IN THE ILLUSION

I SPENT 25 YEARS OF MY CAREER IN THE SELF-HELP/PERSONAL development industry, the majority of which was spent in various security, risk management, stage presenter, operations, medical and safety director, production and engineering roles supporting Tony Robbins. It had enormous, priceless rewards, long stressful hours, many times 21 hours a day, some missed expectations, some unrealistic expectations and a few disappointments. I finally made a critical, well thought out decision to leave and walk my own personal development path, as it became time for me to follow my own destiny and legacy.

Leaving was not simple, but it was necessary and I believe pre-destined. I suffered separation anxiety when I left, as it was a personal and highly valued key part of my life. I had made literally thousands of personal friendships with amazing people worldwide, which magnified the separation anxiety.

My diverse roles allowed me to fulfill the full spectrum of my multi-faceted background, which gave me not only a full sense of purpose and gratitude, but also allowed me to serve at the highest level.

Over the 25 years, I visited so many countries I've lost count. I traveled over 3 million miles on airplanes, and spent so many nights in hotel rooms that it added up to years. I unloaded shipping containers and tractor-trailers, fixed forklifts that broke during loading, redesigned the Robbins warehouse, and designed all the road cases for all the events. At preconvention meetings with hotel or convention center staff, I was often time introduced as Gary King aka, MacGyver. For 14 of those years, I drove Tony in every city in the world where we held events. Many times, I did the impossible with minimal resources and impossible odds. I loved what I did, and loved why I did it.

I did not always agree with practices and policies. Because I have been in leadership roles since I was 14 years old, I see myself as a great leader, not so much a great follower. I lead with my conscience, compassion, courage and common sense.

I was sometimes addressed as "the voice of reason" when situations took on the foundation of chaos due to far too many spokes in the wheel and uncontrollable sets of circumstances.

I also had the honor and privilege to work regularly with participants who did not get their desired emotional void filled. That allowed me to use my own life experiences and 25 years of studying practical psychology to often get the person on a healthy emotional path. There were also times when participants got into major sleep deprivation, dehydration and overwhelm and I had to call 911. It was heartbreaking to say the very least. Apparently, I was born an empath, so I felt more than my share of compassion.

I remember back in the 90s when my birthday fell during an event, and to my surprise, Tony called me to the front of the stage. To my further shock and surprise, he gave me a brand new Harley Sportster for my birthday. He was a tall man with a tall heart.

I also remembered years ago, I had picked him up at a private airport to drive him to his hotel and it was only he and I in the van. I said to him, "Thanks TR, (I called him TR rather than Tony) for saving my life back in 1991". He remarked, "I did not save your life, you did". I then went on to tell him, "Someday TR I'm going to write a book". And he said, "What will it be about?" I replied, "It will be about my life story, and how I overcame the impossible".

I would love to say it was all great, fulfilling and enlightening, but there were some painful moments. I remember sitting on a golf cart late one night at an event in Hawaii with TR when he shared his heart with me. I felt honored and trusted. Soon afterward, he went through a painful divorce. It was painful for me as well, only on a very different level. He divorced his wife Becky Robbins, who was a dear and close friend. It broke my heart to see her go, and I lost touch with her for 11 years. I am extremely grateful that we reconnected after 12 years and I get to continue my treasured friendship with her. You see in my world, people are everything, and money is secondary.

Sometime later, I was invited to Tony and Sage's wedding in Fiji, which was also an honor as I was considered part of the family. At the reception, I was asked if I wanted to stand up and speak, and I said "absolutely". I said, "Tony and Sage, I thought long and hard about an appropriate wedding gift for you both, not easy by any means. I finally thought of the perfect gift, no matter what happens in our lives, I will always unconditionally love you both". There were times I struggled with my promise, and I happy to say, to this day, through thick and thin, I have kept my promise.

My 25-year journey was not without overwhelming heartbreak. When I had just arrived in Australia to load in a Robbins event, I received the most heartbreaking and shocking phone call I had ever received in my life. It was a phone call that changed my life forever. My only biological child, my son, had taken his life while I was traveling to the event. My nephew, Tom Stock, made the call to me, God love him, to this day I have no idea how he got the courage to make that call. I made a really tough decision to stay for the 12-day event to support my team with my event responsibilities, and to have my team support me emotionally at a time of dire desperation. I did my job, and my core team, the Robbins trainers were an unbelievable support team for me.

Then there came my departure day from Australia back to Florida. It surpassed being a nightmare by anyone's standards. I arrived at the Brisbane airport to check in and immediately went into shock. I was flying home to my only child's funeral, which was literally hours after my arrival back home. I stood at the Qantas check in counter and could not even speak. What I'm about to share with you is so far beyond customer service it should be called angel service. The Qantas agent got on the radio and put in motion a whole group of Qantas employees. They walked me by the hand through every procedure. They radioed baggage handlers, pilots, ground crew, and customer service agents. At one point when it looked like I was going to miss my connection from Brisbane to Sydney for the international flight, a flight attendant kneeled on the floor in the aisle and held my hand during the flight. On the International flight, Qantas moved me from coach to Business class complimentary as an act of extreme compassion and generosity. The international flight crew/ customer service manager showed me his office on the plane and told me to get up and walk in anytime during the flight. As I write this, the tears are pouring down my face for the enormous gratitude to Qantas Airlines, and their amazing employees, angels are everywhere.

You see, in life nothing happens by accident. I believe it is all predestined. If it were not for the 25 years in that world, I would not have met Vickie Smith, who made this book possible. She was Tony's personal assistant at the time, and she is now my manager, friend, mentor, angel, support system, and the main and only reason this book is now a reality.

During those 25 years, I paid very close attention to all the interventions, heartbreaking stories, personal issues shared, and the fact that no less than 6 million people were participants over the years. From my observations, interviews and stage presentations I noticed a common void in almost all the attendee's lives. It was from that profound awareness I created the concept for "The Happiness Formula® - The Ultimate Life Makeover™".

When you spend 50% of your career life in a place that is highly-emotionally charged and in many ways extremely addictive, you must go deep inside yourself and allow your intuition, conscience, and faith to be your guide.

The personal development industry is an $11 BILLION a year industry[2]. That is an enormous amount of earned and borrowed capital spent on the hope of personal development. What's the attraction? Why do so many spend so much money on personal development? What exactly are the attendees attempting to develop?

In many cases it boils down to the unsolved mystery of their misunderstood, possibly dysfunctional, or even abusive childhood which is buried in repression and suppression and shows up in adult life as a void to fill. In my hundreds of interviews with participants and audiences, I have determined the real search was not about success at all, it was the search for Happiness, Joy and Fulfillment. People are just conditioned to believe that Happiness is a byproduct of success, when in reality; it is the other way around. True and heartfelt real success is a byproduct of Happiness.

The desire to be a "better person", to live a "happier life" and to help others achieve the same appears to be universal with people who have a strong conscience and live by The Golden Rule: "*Do onto others as you would have them do onto you*".

It goes back to one of the many reasons that I have written this book. It is my legacy to do this. It's my purpose. Otherwise, I would not have spent the equivalent of 40 years of hours in the industry.

For the first ten years, I was caught in the illusion. I own it. I'm accountable for it. I'm not ungrateful. I'm grateful for my experience because I learned a lot. I also gained an awareness that I did not have when I started and I became wiser from the journey.

That's why I created the material that I'm sharing with you. It's out of wisdom. I'm doing this to fill the needs of people who are suffering emotionally and maybe have for a long time; they are looking for answers.

Individually, we each must choose our own paths needed to learn and grow. When I found myself decaying, I knew it was time to get back on the growth path and leave my past in the past. I am very grateful for the gift of travel, never-ending friendships, compensation, and both conditional and unconditional Love. The gift I leave behind is the most important thing I learned in the 25 years; it came from the observations I made, notes I took, and people I listened to and supported. I leave behind "The Happiness Formula®."

Chapter 20

EMOTIONAL IMMUNITY

In general, our westernized lifestyle does not support any of The Happiness Formula elements. Most people do not go around forgiving themselves and other people. Sadly, we have normalized dysfunctional behavior, where lying, cheating and white-collar crime is considered acceptable. Normalizing this behavior gives people permission to reside in a space where they believe this behavior is okay, measuring their life experiences through what the outside world tells them is acceptable.

If when the phone rings, I say, "Tell them I'm not here", then other people will justify it's ok to do that as well. If I step over a piece of paper on the ground, the person behind will do the same. However, if I reach down and pick it up, there is a good chance the person behind will do the same when coming across another on the ground.

It is so empowering, because once you see the responsibility you have, then someone will notice every small thing you do. If what you do is for good, people will take that with them. If it is a negative thing, they will take that with them as well.

As I walk around college campuses, I do not see anything that supports forgiveness, nor anything that supports honesty. There is nothing on campus boards that say, "Nothing is more important than your character." I have found nothing that supports healthy self-worth.

In Anita Moorjanis' amazing book, *Dying To Be Me*, Anita falls prey to her greatest fear, cancer. Ultimately, this devastating disease engulfed her body and she was comatose in a hospital bed when she had a "near death experience" where she experienced unexplainable transcendence. Only minutes later, she received spontaneous healing. Anita realized a profound epiphany, being true to herself would be a major key to a healthy well-lived life.

This book and many others like it poses a deep and perplexing question: How much does our emotional health and balance control our physical health?

I believe it is far more powerful than we can possibly imagine. I predict that in the near future, emotional well-being will set the standard for physical health, well-being and life's longevity.

Chapter 21

NONJUDGMENTAL JUDGMENT

I OPENLY TALK ABOUT CONSULTING WITH THERAPISTS. MANY PEOPLE who need therapy will not go because they fear being judged by their friends. If you need therapy, make an appointment. If you cannot afford it, find a resource to help you pay for it.

I pay a therapist to judge me in a way that is nonjudgmental; a therapist that will point out what is good for me, and what is not.

When you go through psychotherapy, the therapist learns your personality and behavior. It is very easy for a trained psychologist to identify personality disorders when there is no vested emotional interest. It isn't difficult for them to determine what goes on inside a patient, why it happens, what perpetuates it and how to resolve it. While most people do not like to talk about their childhood, most psychotherapists start there.

So, how does nonjudgmental judgment apply to parenting? Often, in my research with audiences, I ask them if they remember when they were punished as a child. As an example: Suppose you have a five-year-old child, and you come home to find that he has taken crayons and written all over the living room wall. You walk into the house and what do you do? What does the average parent do? They get very upset and start yelling at their child, making their child feel like they are wrong, and like they are bad.

What are your expectations? What are you expecting from your child that is not realistic? There are two ways to respond to coming home and seeing crayon marks on the living room wall. One way is you could freak out and scream at your child; or you can walk in the door and say, "Oh my goodness, after seeing what you just did on the living room wall I suspect you're going to be a very famous artist. Everybody is going to know who you are. You'll be very famous." Then you go to the store and buy some paint, wall cleaner, an easel and a big pad that's 3 feet high and 5 feet across, and a whole bunch of markers. Encourage the creativity.

I watched interviews with David Blaine, a very well-known street magician from New York. In the documentary about his childhood, he spoke about the interaction that his mother had with him. It was very interesting because he said she never criticized him. His mother told him was going to be famous. No matter what he did, she encouraged him.

After events, I always stay for questions. At one event, I spoke about parenting and specifically about the writing on the walls, and how it gets translated on a child. A woman was upset, telling me "I was listening to what you were saying and I feel like I've been a bad parent. I have two 7-year-olds and they are constantly fighting with each other."

I asked her, "What is it that you are trying to get them to do? They are 7-year-olds; do you want them to act as if they are 20? So what is it that you think they are doing wrong?"

She replied, "They are misbehaving."

I said, "You mean they are noncompliant? Why do you want them to be compliant? They are twins, and although they are twins, they have different personalities. Is fighting wrong or bad? Are they doing it with hammers, chisels, and axes? Remember they are children. Are you trying to make your children adults when they're children? What does "behave" mean? Is it something that they shouldn't be doing? They are children. You aren't a bad parent."

You likely got your parenting skills from your parents. It is highly unlikely they knew how to parent without judgment. When do you start reacting without judgment and use compassion instead?

CHAPTER 22

HUMAN HEART DEGREE

IN THE 12 YEARS I SPENT IN PUBLIC SCHOOL, AT LEAST SIX OF THEM were wasted. If I were taught self-worth, I could have learned what I needed to in half that time. If you have self-confidence, i.e., self-worth, you can learn much faster because you aren't in fear of making mistakes. You aren't paralyzed with the fear of being judged or rejected. You are not in fear of test scores.

Recently, I read a headline in the Tampa Bay Times that said, in big huge block letters, "36,000 STUDENTS MUST REPEAT". I believe it was third graders who needed to repeat the third grade in the state of Florida because they had not passed the reading test.

Educators would want you to believe it is because many students have ADD. It is boredom because they are not stimulated. The children don't pay attention because the material in public schools isn't stimulating for them. Sadly, for whatever reason, the educational systems have not picked up on this and taken action.

What is the biggest crisis plaguing the educational world currently? Bullying. What is the educational system doing to address bullying? They are being effect-specific. They are doing bullying workshops. They are issuing punishment for bullying. They are trying to manage bullying so it is effect-specific, but managing effects will never solve the problem.

You have to manage the cause. Do healthy self-worth people bully others? No, they don't. Whether one is 14 or 44 years old, low self-worth people tend to bully other people. When I give a presentation to teen groups, one of the first things I talk about is bullying. I ask them, "What is the biggest problem you have in school?", and "Who has the courage to raise your hand and tell me why you bullied someone?" They will often answer me because I make it safe for them to answer. I do not judge their response. Most of them will tell me, "I was afraid. I was scared and that's why I bullied someone."

Are teachers asking these questions?

Another concern is the dropout rate of our students. When I graduated in 1963, I had a graduating class of 450 people and only two dropped out in my graduating class. The dropout rate today is a problem that should no longer be ignored.

So, here's my curiosity. Who is asking the dropouts why they are dropping out, and who is actually listening to them? Who is actually being cause-specific rather than effect-specific? Many teens say they drop out because it was boring, or teachers are mean, or they didn't feel they were learning what they needed relevant to their life.

If you say their reasons are ridiculous, you make them feel small, because the reasons they dropped out are effect-specific. When I cross paths with parents, nearly all say schools today are a train wreck. Schools are broken. Schools are not working. Those who appear happy with schools are parents who have their children in private or charter schools. I take this information to heart. When I discuss education, a few parents will state that it's not the responsibility of the school to teach self-worth. That it should be taught in the home. That is a great idea and would work in a perfect world, but what happens to the children whose parents don't have the skills or desire to teach healthy self-worth? In many families, the parent's primary focus is in trying to figure out how to survive, how to pay the bills and have something left over to buy school supplies or take the kids to the movies.

I am often invited to speak in schools, and I realize not all families are faced with situations like that, but there are way too many of them that are. I went to speak at a local school and I was told in advance the school is full of "at risk" students. Along with the dropout rate increase and the need for "at risk" schooling, bullying and drug use increases. Who is doing something about it? Who is researching the cause, instead of putting a band-aid on the effects?

It's just more of the same, cramming more academics and more intense testing, to get better funding based on test scores. What does that nonsense produce? I have parents tell me their kids are overly stressed and can't sleep at night because of the constant and intense testing. Teachers have been told that if their students don't do well enough in state and federal testing, it affects their salary. What are the state administrators thinking?

Making children's performance on tests tied to teacher salary and school funding, is nonsense. I know most teachers are very compassionate at what they do. There are dedicated teachers who want to overcome the issues. But the curriculum says, "No way. You cannot deviate from the curriculum."

What happened to the educational process that says the definition of education is to bring out the best in a child?

The best solution that I can see starts in the public schools. I suggest this experiment: A tenth-grade teacher draws a line on the chalkboard and writes six or seven traits of low self-worth on one side of the line and she writes six or seven traits of healthy self-worth on the other side of the line.

She allows them five minutes to look at the chalkboard and lets them know if they are interested in pursuing additional information about self-worth there are a few books they can read. She then lets them know there's a stack of them in the back of the room or they can get it in the school library and they are free to take one copy for a month to read. Teachers should be trained and have access to these books:

1. *Forgive for Good,* by Dr. Fred Luskin
2. *The 10 Days to Self Esteem,* by David Burns
3. *Just Be Honest,* by Steven Gaffney

Try it in one school and see what happens. At the end of the school year, for the participating 10th grade, there would be measurable results.

Would there be tests on those books? Absolutely not. However, there would be an open discussion led by the teacher who had also read the books and understands the value of forgiveness and self-worth. If that experiment was repeated in 9th, 11th and 12th grade, the kind of person graduating the high school would be different.

As Malcolm Gladwell states,

"It's the smallest things that create the biggest shifts."

Looking back, what have I actually used from 12 years of public education? What have I put to use that has a practical application in my lifetime? I know how to read. I have read more than 2200 books. I learned how to write and do basic math. Academically, I knew where my strengths were and I knew where my weaknesses were. I didn't try to make my weaknesses into strengths; I tried to make my strengths even stronger. In my time, I had a unique situation in that by the end of my junior year, I already had enough credits to graduate. I convinced the guidance counselor to give me two periods of shop class because I like to work with my hands. Memorizing poems had no practical application to me. Yes, I'm a public speaker. I speak extemporaneously. I did not learn that in school. I graduated in 1963, and the very day I graduated, I went to work as an auto mechanic. I was self-actualized. I came to the conclusion that I could learn to do anything by watching someone else do it properly.

As I reflect on my time in public school, what was the takeaway? Obviously, I took away the high school experiences, the parties, the friends, and all those kinds of things. But practically, what did I gain? Do I remember the poems I had to memorize? No. I think 20 percent of my 12 years of education applied to my adult life.

The Happiness Formula (Forgiveness, Honesty and Truth, and Self Worth) should be taught in schools. If any school system had taken the time to teach these elements, it is quite likely my life choices and my life decisions would have been completely different. My relationship decisions would have been different.

When I went to public school, I was starving to death for something I couldn't intellectually understand. I was starving for somebody to say something that gave me an insight or perspective - anything about life, other than learning algebra or memorizing sentence structure. I was just there. I couldn't intellectualize. I was starving.

In Copenhagen, the woman transporting me from the airport to a high school, said, "The headmaster told me to warn you about two things. Number one, the kids are going to be rude to you. Number two, you'll never be able to hold their attention for more than 30 minutes." My reply was "I leave my ego at the door." I've been doing this a long time.

Typically, when I finish a presentation, I'm often asked to stay longer. I've never had a teenager be rude to me during my presentations. Never. I've never had kids want to leave before I finished, because they are starving for this insight. The things that I say just happen to be the things that they're starving for. It's what I starved for.

If you have a room full of kids, chances are the vast majority are single parent kids, or they are stress income kids. After spending this time with a group of teens, the adults will come and ask me who I am. Their children talk to them about me, telling them what I've told them, shared with them, questions I asked them. I tell them I don't have a teaching degree. I have a human heart degree.

Sir Ken Robinson is an amazing man, with amazing material and knows how to capture an audience. He has a 12-minute video called "*Do Schools Kill Creativity?*" His presentations are so thought provoking, because 90% of them are common sense logic.

Our schools teach brain stuff, not heart stuff. Current society thinks that teaching brain stuff somehow guarantees some sort of life success. That is not reality.

The educational process reinforces low self-worth in many ways. This doesn't mean there's no value in the education process. It just means you get an education based on testing, memorizing, and academic information. Academic information doesn't have any bearing on your emotional life other than your career path. Schools teach children about success. The problem is they don't explain to them actually what success is.

Schools teach that the goal is to be successful, and success comes from education, which creates a career, which equals success. Supposedly, that career equals some sort of financial fulfillment that supposedly equals emotional fulfillment. If that were accurate, you wouldn't see the results we have in this country and the world today. If those things were real, and academics were a foundation for emotional stability and emotional well-being, at some point, would equal inner peace and happiness.

My comment about the education system is contextual, not every student enters with low self- worth and not every student leaves with low self-worth.

My research, my intelligence and my practical experience speaking in schools tell me that in most cases, the education system is severely broken. It does not fit the definition of education, which is to bring out the best in the child. In my opinion, this should be the actual definition of education. In many cases, they stir up and feed low self-worth by the process. They are taught that academics are the pathway to a quality life. It lacks any foundation of common sense to think that academics are the entire foundation for quality life.

Since I often speak to groups of children and teens, I receive emails and private messages that would break your heart. Some teens in Holland have asked me to come there and speak, as the suicide rate in schools is up 400% in the last four years.

Here is an unedited email that I received:

"Mr King,

I find it disappointing that I'm writing this. I've spent my whole life, so far, in schooling that has been affecting me as an individual in a way I see as generally dull and disappointing. I'm tired of wasting my time, in an environment that is conforming me and my beliefs, verses nurturing my individuality, & diversity. I would love to not just know how to structure a paper, and do calculus, but also how to come up with my own opinion, and learn what it means to really back it up and defend it, or create something beautiful for my personal fulfillment. That shouldn't be taught in an elective class, but rather required, so my peers, and myself could gain more confidence and respect for ourselves and each other.

Children are like sponges, and I'm positive you've heard that a million times. But obviously many teachers are not keeping that in mind. Since sixth grade most of my teachers don't seem excited to be in their classrooms. Psychologically, this sets an example of what students expect with learning. When students don't expect their teachers to be excited to teach, or don't expect to learn anything they will not find the motivation or inspiration to learn. Plain and simple. Even worse they might begin to believe that they have nothing else to learn. So when the teacher stands in front of the room for a lecture, or to help with students notes, the students will not consume the information well. They can't learn if they are not in the correct mind set. Ultimately this is destructive for every person in the class, including the teacher.

As students we have also become afraid to take risks, and ask questions.

As we spend more time in the classroom, being told we're wrong, and being taught things that we're to comfortable with, we become accustomed to not ask questions or do things outside of the box. This is becoming an extreme problem, as technology continues To influence, not just the way students find and memorize the information for their classes, but also how they communicate. Kids my age (teens) expect information and change for their personal benefit immediately. Eventually kids will find themselves thinking they aren't capable of thinking or doing anything worthy for their society, or peers. Students quickly begin to associate school with negative thoughts, and they find the environment of their school to controlling. Every day students are ecstatic to leave school as soon as that bell rings.

At the end of each and every school year we find more young adults And kids being depressed, tired, overworked, and at a lack of motivation to shape their future. It's definitely time to invest more time and effort into education not just in America, but really everywhere, so that we can leave not just a legacy, but help those younger than us to do the same. If we want our children, and our children's children to be proud and passionate about that they do, let's help them by starting at the source.

Devin,

16 year old high school student"

If I were asked to design the curriculum for public schools, the three most important changes I would make are:

1. No Testing
2. No Homework
3. Most importantly, Teach 50% academics and 50% life skills.

I would like to use school buses for a greater purpose. There are 480,000 school buses in the United States, and they all say the same thing, the district it serves. I would put on the side of the bus: **Your Character is Our Future**, or **Nothing Is More Important Than Your Character**, or **Real Winners Never Cheat**.

Not only students, but also adults would see these school buses as well. It is behavior reinforcement. The reason school buses are yellow with black lettering is because it is the most effective way to visually get a message into the brain.

Chapter 23

STARVING TO FIND SELF WORTH

THE PRISON POPULATION IN THE UNITED STATES IS HORRIFIC. Frankly, prisons now in the U.S. are nothing but huge financial ventures, and that's why private companies are buying and building prisons.

On the outskirts of downtown Dublin, Ireland, there are three prisons: the men's prison, the women's prison and a teen prison. I once spoke at Mount Joy, a Men's Medium Security Prison in Dublin, Ireland. I believe the prison was built to hold 500 people, but it was over populated at 550. It was a dungeon built in 1857 by the British. The cells didn't have bars on them. They were solid concrete, like a tomb, with a solid steel door with a peephole in it.

When I spoke there, they did something with me they don't typically do. Rather than be limited to only the Visitor's Center, they took me to the main cellblock, which is five stories tall with railings and a common area in the center. The jailer opened a big locking bar door and told me he was going to introduce me to a prisoner who is on a life sentence, and asked if it would be okay to lock me in. Of course, I said, "Absolutely!"

I shook the prisoner's hand, and he told me, "Every day I pray to God, to give me the strength to live another day. Every day I pray to God that somebody will just listen while I talk." So I stood there and listened to him talk about his daughters, and how he wanted so badly to see them. No matter how often he was told he could see them, it never happened.

Two other prisoners walked up and joined us. One asked me, "Do you know that five days ago, one of our friends was stabbed to death right there?", as he pointed to a place on the floor six feet from where we were standing.

Later, the jailer had a personal conversation with me telling me, "I have no proof of this, but I suspect many, if not all of the prisoners have suffered some sort of abuse at some point in their lives."

I spoke at Dochas Centre, a Women's Prison, on the same piece of property. It was the only day of the year when all the women in the prison were in one room at the same time, because they had completed a Breast Cancer Walk around the exercise yard. I observed that most of the women there were under 35 years old. I looked in their eyes. I could look right through them. They were hollow.

A friend who went with me pointed to two women, telling me, "They are sisters. One is 27 and the other is 31. They are called the 'Scissor Sisters', and are famous here in Ireland. They are in for life."

The next day, I spoke there. In prison, they can't force the prisoners to listen to a speaker. It's by choice. I went to the room, and the women started to show up. I was about ten minutes into my talk when I was pleasantly surprised to see the "Scissor Sisters" show up to hear what I had to say. At one point, I noticed that one of the sisters was crying, and to me those tears meant my words entered her heart. At the end of the presentation one of the women asked if I would come to lunch with them. Though not part of the plan, the jailer approved the request.

On the way to the cafeteria, a 26-year-old woman asked me, "Mr. King, can you tell me how to get someone to love me?" As it turns out, she was referring to her mother, who never visited or communicated with her so far during her eight-year sentence. I told her, "You need to unconditionally love your mother, expecting nothing in return. Do not expect her to visit or write to you. Just love her." As a result, she wrote a letter to her mother and over time, practicing unconditional love, her mother started to visit. They became friends and eventually they allowed her a one-day furlough to go into the city with her mother. If I remember correctly, her sentence was reduced due to good behavior.

There is no substitute for unconditional love.

The entire prison population, both men and women, is full of low self-worth people. Those with high self-worth don't go to prison. Nearly every crime is low self-worth related, but they don't teach prisoners how to achieve healthy self-worth. Do people with high self-worth have addiction issues? Not typically. Do people with high self-worth rob stores? Not typically.

I primarily speak about forgiveness when speaking at prisons. I do so because everyone in there, no matter why they are there, has huge forgiveness issues that need addressed. While they are incarcerated, they go through many emotions, including sadness, loss and grief.

Many don't understand the value that comes from connecting soul to soul with another person without judgment. I've been asked to speak in prisons numerous times, and plan to do even more of that because there's enormous value to both myself and those I speak with.

CHAPTER 24

DISTRACTION

RIGHT NOW, THE WORLD IS AT A VERY VULNERABLE, TEETERING POINT. In my lifetime, I've never seen a time when so much fear is marketed in this country. The main product is fear, and it is displayed instantaneously via the internet, television and movies. When I grew up, there was no mechanism to receive instantaneous news or feedback. You might not learn of an event for a month. Now there are psychologists who say handheld communication devices will ultimately destroy the world.

When I do teen presentations, I joke with the kids and bring out my flip phone causing them to laugh. They think it's crazy that I have a flip phone rather than an iPhone or some super phone thing where you can dial up the moon with it or whatever. It is a great servant and it is a really bad master.

In a lot of ways, smart phones are what I call "battery powered cocaine". I'm telling you that you possess something that can be the world's greatest tool or it could be the world's greatest piece of destruction. You have to decide where and how it fits into your life.

If my phone rings while I'm having a conversation, I don't stop to answer it. They say, "Uh, your phone is ringing. You're not answering it?"

My reply is always, "Yes I'm aware my phone is ringing. I'm not answering because I'm having a conversation with you not with my phone." How many people do that? Not many.

In grocery or hardware stores, or post office and Walmart, I will often see people go through the checkout line, all while talking on their phone. When it's my turn to check out, I always ask the checkout person, "Excuse me, I'm curious. The person in front of me talked on the phone the whole time. I'm doing research, how did you feel?" Every single person I've ever asked said they found it disgusting they'd do that. They have no self-respect. It's awful.

I fly a lot and I am typically in first class, not because I buy a first class ticket but because of my status in air miles. The entire flight I find that everyone is on a laptop. That is the very last thing I want to do. I just close my eyes and relax in self-care.

No sooner than the wheels touch the tarmac, all the cell phones come out, and people are resuming phone conversations. Thirty-five people can hear all about their garden, the game from last night, the flat tire, etc. I see people try to put their luggage in the overhead while they are balancing their phone on their shoulder talking. Almost always, a flight attendant has to come back multiple times as the plane is taxiing to take off, asking people to stop using their phone. I see they are online during the flight with their laptop, tablet or phone. There isn't a day that goes by I don't see people texting while driving, swerving into other lanes. At stoplights, the first thing people reach for are their phones, to answer a text.

We are technologically supreme and emotionally deficient. We've managed to expand technology, and it almost has the opposite effect on human emotional behavior. People have become so dependent on electronic devices they don't know how to communicate effectively without it. How many times I've walked into a restaurant where a family is having lunch and not one word is said. All are texting from the moment they sit down until the moment they leave. Sadly, this is a very common occurrence.

I was in a restaurant a few months ago and two women walked in during happy hour. I was there for 45 minutes and the entire time, one of the women was on a cell phone and the other was texting. They came in together, so I'm assuming they were friends but they never said one word to each other. When I left, the one was still on the phone and the other one was still texting.

Do you find yourself doing the same thing? If so, perhaps it's time to consider why you feel the need to avoid direct communication.

CHAPTER 25

WHAT THE WORLD NEEDS

I WAS IN ATLANTA, GEORGIA FOR A ROBBINS EVENT A FEW YEARS AGO, my team and I checked into a major hotel chain that was on a busy highway only a few blocks from the convention center where we were having the event. At the time, I was Director of Security.

I met with the hotel manager on local security issues, and he warned me to make sure and tell the team not to walk to the venue alone; it was not safe, as there were many armed robberies on that road in broad daylight. He told me to tell the team to walk in groups, and I passed the information along.

Several days later, without thinking, I set off to walk to the venue alone. Across from the highway was a wooded area, and out of my peripheral vision I saw a very large man bolt out of the woods, run directly across the highway right in my path. He stood two feet from my face; arms folded and said, "I need money".

I simply asked him, "What do you need money for?" and he said, "For my mother".

As I kept asking him questions, he began to relax his arms back to his side. He shared with me that he was a Vietnam Vet and nobody appeared to care. I asked him a few more personal questions, and I was shocked at what happened next. He looked at me and said, "Would you consider giving me a hug?" I stood on the side of the highway hugging that man for several minutes. He then said "Thank You" and ran back across the highway into the woods.

Was I afraid of the man? No, and he knew it. I looked into his eyes, and he looked into mine.

I will let you decide: Was he armed? Was he there to rob me? Was he there to hurt me? Or was he really there because he was hurt, and nobody cared? Well, I think God had us meet that day, and we both got our needs met in a very special way.

CHAPTER 26

YOU HAVE A CHOICE

AS A HUMAN BEING, YOU HAVE A CHOICE IN LIFE. YOU CAN EITHER:

» Be authentic or be inauthentic.

» You can be real, or you can be deceitful/deceptive.

People deceive others to get what they want from them: Love, acceptance, validation, sex, money, rescue and more. So, if you pursue another based on what the other person can give you, what you can get from them, how they validate you, how they can make you feel better about yourself, how to be finally loved by someone – if that's how you're living, the chances of being successful in your pursuit is nonexistent.

Relationships are like icebergs. You cannot see 90% of the iceberg, only the tip. When people meet, they show only the tip of their iceberg and do not reveal what's hidden below. Their connection is based only on allowing the person to see what they make visible. What can result of relationships formed like that? The Titanic. They sink. If you only expose 10% of yourself, you are choosing not to make yourself emotionally available, you decide to disguise your flaws, and you choose to cover up when asked how many times you've been married, and honestly answer the question, "who ended the last relationship you were in?".

Suppose you had a business concept and knew the idea was a home run but needed a business partner to pull it off. You would likely conduct extensive research on prospective partners, doing background checks, viewing their online persona, their creditworthiness, and performing intensive interviews.

Romantic relationships should be approached with more due diligence than just relying on whether they are physically attractive, tells you what you think you want to hear, whether you "feel good" around them or whether there is great sexual chemistry. All that is great, but if you don't consider the 90% that's hidden; it won't be a sustainable relationship.

A friend of mine started his relationship with love, passion, and lust, which then turned into hatred. No one has an answer when asked, "How did you get from love and passion to anger and hate?" It got that way because something about it at the very beginning wasn't conducive to a long-term, healthy, thriving, growing, nurturing, safe relationship. Something was missing at the very start.

If the right elements are there, they will compound. If you start a relationship accepting the white lies someone tells you, those white lies will compound into far more damaging and hurtful lies, like what occurs with affairs. That's how life works. These are basic principles. There's no rocket science and there's no brain surgery in any of this. It is just basic, common behavior. You must understand how you work and how other people work.

I can remember entering into a relationship and having the woman ask me how I felt about her. That was the question. "How do you feel about me?" I looked at her, and I said, "I can't even explain how I feel about myself to you, much less explain to you how I feel about you. I don't even understand me."

Yes, that didn't go over very well at all, but it was the absolute truth. I didn't understand me. Here I am, I couldn't make a marriage work,

I had been in and out of relationships for years, and you can't make a relationship work if you don't have a healthy relationship with yourself.

If you get into a relationship with somebody who has low self-worth, they're simply not emotionally available. They tell lies, and you think you are immune to those lies because love is present. They will lie to others and be deceptive. If you think you are immune to it, you're in denial and out of touch with reality. People who lie, lie. That's what they do. The only thing that separates YOU from the lie is nothing. It just depends on the amount of leverage that occurs to cause the person to be deceptive.

I lacked self-worth, and my expectation of the marriage was that my wife would give me healthier self-worth by the fact that she chose me and married me. By choosing me, I thought I must be likeable, loveable, good, and all these other wonderful things. If that were true, it would be called, "other-worth," not self-worth, or self-esteem. It would be called other-esteem.

If someone has an affair with a married person, then they, as well as the married person has no self-worth. Their inner dialogue deceives them into thinking, "Wow, I must be something else if a married man/woman wants me. I must be good. I must be valuable. I must be likable. I must be lovable." It's the exact same game and it takes two to play it. It isn't one-sided. It's driven by filling emotional needs that the person doesn't know how to fill any other way but externally.

CHAPTER 27

REFLECTION

TO LIVE A LIFE WELL LIVED REQUIRES A NEED TO REFLECT ON THE past so that suppressed and repressed emotions that deplete the natural need for growth and expansion can be resolved. Worldwide, a very high percentage of people experience emotional suppression and repression. Essentially, suppression is the conscious denial of a past event, and repression is the unconscious memory of a past event.

In the human quest for Happiness and fulfillment, it is essential to address these conditions because they commonly go against any chance of inner peace and happiness.

Most people avoid memories of pain and suffering as an emotional survival mechanism. With the right approach, they are also an enormous gift to release the emotional prison that many constantly experience, and consequently use distraction, diversion, addiction and a host of other external means to avoid transcendence.

They allow their life to be controlled by "cognitive dissonance" which is simply defined as the human justification for all behavior, which includes, lying, cheating, stealing, addictions, criminal behavior, illegal, dangerous and a host of other self and other destructive behavior.

As I reflect upon a lifetime of "on and off" horrific pain and suffering, I discovered the "cause", which translates to human emotional resolve. Almost all of the causes of pain and suffering were a result of repression or suppression. Because my PTSD started at fivc years old and then compounded throughout my life, I was determined to find a solution to my personal suffering that would allow me the ability to help others.

Although PTSD is typically associated with returning Military, it is also a wide spread common emotional illness within any population. Unfortunately, it goes undiagnosed in far too many lives.

As a result of my own reflection and years of research, I will share with you what is known as the "Top five regrets in the last hours of a person's life".

These are not in any particular order, but they are all profound and life changing, if you choose to make internal shifts that create short and long-term resolve, inner peace and Happiness.

I wish I would have had the courage to share my true feelings, rather than suppress them in order to keep the peace and be a pleaser. The end result of suppressing feelings causes resentment, which can translate into physical disease.

I wish I would have been true to myself, rather than living a life others expected of me, causing me to somehow justify my choices, and getting caught in the trap of thinking that being true to myself was "selfish", as used in a negative context. Being true to yourself is NOT selfish, it is called "self-care". One of the major lessons I learned in therapy was, "Always practice self-care".

I wish I would not have worked so long and so hard, especially doing things I did not like and had no true passion for the process or outcome. It also screams of "cognitive dissonance", the justification to work rather than being a great relationship partner and a great parent. It also speaks to the workaholic who while working all day long is thinking, "I should be home with my family", and then when home with the family is thinking, "I should be working". The reality is the person is self-destructive while destroying the outside world as well.

I wish I would have spent more time with my friends. This was a strong reality check for me. What was the justification for overlooking long time friendships? Why did I choose to not forgive my past lovers and partners so that we could be long-time friends? Why did they not forgive me? Why did I get so obsessed with achievements, materialism, conquests, and distractions, that I forgot the heart connections that were far more important than stuff? When I left the 25-year worldwide journey working in the personal development industry as road manager, I fell into "separation anxiety" due to the disconnection from hundreds if not thousands of interpersonal relationships and treasured friendships. The suffering I experienced was NOT related to the 25-year loss of income. It is also why in the front of this book I created a list of people I could remember that have added value to my life, many of which have long since passed away, but not in my heart. There are also hundreds of others that added huge value, if you're not on the list, I guarantee you, you are in my heart.

I wish I would have given myself permission to be happy. Yes, Happiness is a **choice**. It is NOT a person, place or thing. It comes from a place of inner peace, not outer trappings. "Trappings" is an interesting descriptive, as it indicates being trapped or imprisoned by the external world. Almost every overly wealthy individual I know is "faking happiness" to be politically correct, and because I suspect they feel the need prove internally "the means always justify the ends". This is the perfect "cognitive incongruent life" rather than a life well lived with no regrets.

As you reflect on your own life, and the above five most common world-wide life regrets, do you happen to notice there is no reference to money, power, materialism, soul mates, conquests, winning the lottery(which statistically does more damage than good), exotic cars, jewelry, 15,000 sq. ft. houses, yachts, or private jets?

In the profound words of Tom Shadyac, the producer of the Jim Carey movies and others, *"I had it all WRONG"*, which lead him to produce the movie *I Am* in 2010.

Reflection is a gift, not a punishment. To understand emotional cause creates resolve to stop managing effects that will never bring you inner peace. For the first time since I was five years old, I have been released from an emotional prison that was created by repression and suppression.

I no longer have to prove anything to anyone for any reason. I know that no one has done anything to me, and that everything that has happened is because of me. The translation of the last statement is I'm 100% accountable, which means I'm 100% free. While many of my choices were subconscious choices, they were not mistakes because ultimately they caused me to push the "reset button".

What is the reset button? Reflection, motive, self-care, understanding the laws of cause and effect, quality therapy including hypnosis, and the constant practice of "The Happiness Formula®" .

CHAPTER 28

EMOTION MANAGEMENT

HOW DO PEOPLE GET THEMSELVES IN A POSITION WHERE THEY become desensitized to the human heart and soul? When are you no longer sensitive to deception, lying and cheating? How do you get there? It's not accidental. At some point in your life, and perhaps it happens over a very long period of time, but you were influenced to believe that deception is normal, correct and required. You may have also been led to believe that deception has an upside and that being honest has a downside.

If you are making relationship choices and you have an operating system that's based on low self-worth, you believe you are unlovable, bad, wrong and not enough. It's subconscious, not conscious, although it lives in the conscious mind as well. When you go out into the world with low self-worth, who are you choosing? Often, someone with low self-worth.

If you have a history of emotional abuse, you will likely do one of two things: You will be an emotional abuser or you will be emotionally abused.

In psychology, it is a well-known fact that a lot of emotionally abused people become emotional abusers themselves. Why? It's creating an operating system. They do it, hate themselves for doing it, then they do it again and hate themselves again for doing it. Each time, they drive their self-worth even lower.

To solve any life problem, you must first acknowledge the problem.

- You can't solve anything if you're in denial.
- You can't solve anything if you don't know what you don't know.

The management of human emotion is the key to leading an emotionally healthy life. You can make all the money you want. Believe me, I know many people with millions of dollars who can spend $10,000 a day and never run out of money. I've studied why people behave the way they do and the majority of those who thrive on financial success never find inner peace, because the drive itself toward achieving financial success is the addiction that is never satisfied. The addiction is supposed to lead to some internal fulfillment, joy and peace, but in reality, it leads to internal chaos because it can never be satiated. If you're driven by power and money, you will never have enough to make you happy and content. You'll never have enough power or money to sit still and watch the clouds and not have to produce something or take some kind of action.

If you choose to live your life that way, you'll get to the end of it and realize, "I think I missed something along the way." I've been down this path, and I've made a lot of money in my lifetime and I've thrown a lot of it away. I went completely broke, and I couldn't buy food or pay my taxes.

There is so much wisdom in Napoleon Hill and his famous *Think and Grow Rich* book. Hill was hired by Carnegie to study the traits of successful people and what they did to become successful. People who struggled the most to achieve success were the ones who valued that success more, truly learning from that struggle. Those who had success handed to them, never became wise from their success. They became driven by it.

CHAPTER 29

CRITICAL DECISIONS

YOUR CIRCUMSTANCES NEVER CONTROL YOUR EMOTIONS AND YOUR future. Your choices do.

In my life, I have made thousands of critical decisions, many of which contained enormous risk. I raced both motorcycles and drag cars, and spent sixteen years as a professional powerboat race driver. Each foot of every lap around a three-mile course, traveling across water at speeds exceeding 120 miles per hour, dealing with oil slicks or rain on a track, and waves or wakes from other boats all require a critical decision to be made.

As an international professional sand sculpting artist, I have created sculptures up to 60 feet in height, requiring thousands of tons of sand. One false move could have buried me, or at the least embarrassed me in front of the Presidential Press Corp and nationwide television networks. I performed for President Clinton in 1995, and shortly after at Disney World, and knew one wrong decision would be professional failure in front of the media.

For 35 years, I was the Executive Event Producer and Race Director for motorsports events, managing a staff of 2,000, crowds between

50,000 and 200,000, 175 paramedics who were standing by, helicopters in the air while cars and boats traveled dangerous speeds. Every decision made was critical because many lives hung in the balance.

For 12 years, I was the Director of Security and Road Manager for well-known celebrities worldwide, entrusted with their personal safety and well-being in all types of uncontrolled situations. One wrong decision and someone's life was in danger. In these circumstances, a decision once made, could not often be changed.

During the last four years of my life, I have had to make the most critical personal decisions I have ever had to make. I had to reach deep inside my heart and soul to search for a meaning so powerful, it would overwhelm a life of routine suffering and depression, lost love, and inferiority complexes that were well beyond complex.

This book is that meaning I decided upon, my most critical decision to date. Although I have studied human behavior and psychology for more than thirty years, I was unable to be my own therapist under the given set of circumstances. I chose to do what many people would never choose. I required the quality emotional support of three highly trained psychologists and psychotherapists. They are not only experts; they are brilliant in every sense of the word. They paved the way to save myself from myself. Each of the three complemented the other, which created exponential growth and enormous insights into a life long struggle.

Because I had a raging case of PTSD, I started with a psychologist trained in EMDR, a method of creating brain resolve for circumstances that surpass the brain's normal function.

I started by contacting Francine Shapiro, the creator of EMDR therapy in the 1980s, and asked for a list of therapists in the Tampa Bay area. I chose Dr. Thomas E. Petit Ph.D., L.M.H.C. and spoke with his wife Ruthie, who listened to the short version of a life-long tale of pain and suffering. Realizing the severity of my case, they juggled clients to immediately get me back-to-back appointments.

They were very clear about my risk factor, as I was as well and Dr. Petit exceeded all of my expectations. No matter how much fear and anxiety I was experiencing, when I walked out of his office, I felt enormous relief in being able to manage the PTSD.

The EMDR treatment with Dr. Petit helped clear much of the trauma, identify and moderate triggers while increasing my capacity for self-regulation. Longstanding and deeply rooted lies about my self-worth began to give way to the truth.

My next self-appointed step to correct the life-long emotional challenges of lack of self-worth was to find a psychotherapist who was also a clinical hypnotherapist. I knew for many years, that 90% of all human behavior is subconscious, and only 10% is under your direct control. As fate and faith had it, I discovered Dr. Shay Roop in Clearwater, Florida who was exactly the right person with the right skills. To say she is brilliant is a huge understatement. I have had numerous cognitive therapy and hypnosis sessions with her, and because of my psychology background, she would occasionally remind me "I am the therapist here." It was exactly what I wanted and needed to hear. Dr. Shay taught me simple strategies such as the importance of practicing self-care, as well as more complex understandings such as the "love map". It has been a priceless journey. With every session, I grew emotionally, physically and spiritually.

Once when Dr. Shay was unavailable, she suggested I meet with her husband, Dr. Rob Roop, also a psychotherapist. He was direct with me, something I greatly appreciated. I joked with him that I would tell my friends, "Look, I pay for the therapists to hand me my lunch box. I do not want to be told what they think I want to hear. That isn't going to help me." In three sessions, Dr. Bob got to the origin of a life-long struggle. I felt as if I could finally breathe and throw the emotional anchor away for good.

Having quality emotional resources is not just a destination plan. It is a journey of self- realization. To me, these three professionals are divine gifts sent to facilitate miracles.

Over time, I have attempted to refer several of my close friends who are suffering to see one of these three angels. They have made critical decisions that have kept them from having a life well lived, and although I've offered to pay for the therapy from the Gary King Foundation. They often turned the help down.

Saving yourself from yourself is an enormous undertaking that requires 100% commitment and resources. The ability to save someone from themselves is practically impossible, but never stop trying to help those who cannot see the forest for the surrounding trees.

There are those who have been struggling with life-long destructive issues who believe therapy is a waste of money and time, thinking they can handle any situation thrown at them with only the emotional support of those who have vested emotional interest in them such as lovers, friends, and family.

Think about it: The average high-end multi-day personal development seminar runs about $15,000. When you factor out of pocket costs including airfare, hotel and meals, it can add another $5,000. That far exceeds the cost of 160 high-quality therapy sessions with long-term sustainable benefits as opposed to attending a seminar consisting primarily of hype and up-sells.

Typically, long-term sustainable change can happen as a result of reversing the personality and character disorders, i.e., abandonment, insecurity, inferiority, low self-worth, addiction, lying and integrity issues. Personally, I have never seen long-term personal or character disorders become reversed at a personal development seminar or event, only short-term euphoric gratification. I say this based only on my personal and professional opinion as a speaker and author, and it is not a blanket statement by any means.

CHAPTER 30

WE ARE GIFTED. WE ARE LIMITLESS.

WE ARE MIRACLES ON TWO LEGS. WE ARE ONE OF THE MOST COMPLEX operating systems on the planet, but we have not been taught how to optimize ourselves. We have been taught how to memorize poems and equations, but not about how to achieve or maintain healthy self-worth. So we always have to question, are we good enough? Are we attractive enough? Are we intelligent enough?

I have two core belief systems. The first is that I can excel at anything as long as I have passion and belief behind it. I can be whatever I want, and be great at anything I choose. The only thing that creates limitations to that statement are the limitations I put on it.

My second core belief is that there is no ending to us, only transformation. I believe you are going to be surprised at what happens. I have done more eulogies than I ever wanted for close friends, and rarely will you ever hear me refer to them as having "passed away". I usually say, "My friend graduated with honors." You graduate, you move on, and you do it again. You learn what you didn't the last time around. When you have no longer have to come back to learn the lessons, you then have a choice of coming back to help other people learn what they need to learn. You could call it being an angel or call it whatever you want, but it is my belief that you come back to help people on their own paths.

Right after my near-death experience, I sat and watched ants for 20 minutes and was fascinated. I would take the time to watch birds fly, enjoying the innocence we were both with and finding everything fascinating. As children, we crawled on our hands and knees, picking little objects out of the carpet because they were fascinating. At some point, we became complacent, and began taking everything for granted; the trees, flowers, water, rain. As I record this chapter, it is pouring rain. I am certain many people are complaining they will get wet if they venture outside, but I would bet there are many more people who would give anything to be able to walk in the rain and get soaking wet because they are lying in a hospital bed or nursing home.

We lose the joy of living our lives because we allow ourselves to be caught up in negative emotions like rejection or anger, choosing to work at jobs we don't have a passion for or want to do, and trading our precious time for money and health insurance.

What would you do if you could do anything?

Why are you doing things you don't want to do?

I have fought my way through most of my life, but I am choosing to live. Really live. I am going on a journey and never allowing the difficult times to make me into a victim. Never. I am victorious.

People have asked me, "If I've been told I have a year left, what would you tell me to do?" Well, the first thing I would say is "Do you believe that is true?" Then I would say that no matter whether that statement is true or false, I would start living my life like it was never going to end. And I do.

The Formula Explained

$F_2HT_2SW=HF^{10}$

F: The F stands for Forgiveness. The 2 means it has 2 parts. You must forgive yourself and others. DO NOT make up reasons why you can't or won't. This is self-destructive.

HT: The H stands for Honesty. The T is for Truthful. The HT also has 2 parts. You need to be Honest with yourself and Truthful with others – NO exceptions. White lies are still lies with consequences.

SW: SW stands for Self-Worth, which is what controls all of life. You either have healthy self-worth, or you have questionable self-worth. If you have questionable self-worth, you cannot forgive or be honest.

HF: HF stands for Happiness and Fulfillment to the power of 10. It is based on the law of compounding and the law of cause and effect.

The lack of Forgiveness, Honesty, Truth and Self Worth is rapidly reaching critical mass in our society. When these elements are totally absent from an individual's life, a leader's life, a country's life, they will be totally absent in the world. When they are totally absent in the world, the quality of life as we know it will disappear. It is happening now.

Chapter 31

STEP 1: FORGIVENESS

CONSIDER THE FOUNDATION OF LIFE AT THE PHYSICAL LEVEL. Physically, the fundamental basics of all human life are food, shelter and clothing. Now, consider the fundamentals of life at an emotional level.

After 30 years of study, I have come to the determination that at the foundation of a human's emotional life is the decision to forgive or not to forgive, to be honest or not to be honest, and your circumstances around your self-worth. These three are the basis for The Happiness Formula®, The Ultimate Life Makeover™.

Most people live wanting something they currently do not have, thinking that once acquired, it will, in some way, produce happiness, joy and bring them inner peace. Numerous studies from psychologists and therapists reveal that the pursuit of happiness is directly linked to a foundation of character, ethics, integrity and morals. Fame and fortune have very little, if anything, to do with true happiness. Being wealthy and having many material possessions is not associated with being happy, having inner peace or joy in one's life.

Everything has a formula; from the air you breathe, to the water you drink. So does happiness. The components of The Happiness Formula®

do not have to be in a particular order as each component is equally important.

The F^2 in The Happiness Formula® stands for two aspects of Forgiveness: Forgiving yourself and forgiving other people. One cannot understate the power of forgiveness. Forgiveness is linked to your immune system, your ability to respond, be responsible, and be response-able.

I liken it to purification of water. No matter how many things you add to a glass of water to make it pure, it will only become pure when you remove its impurities. In other words, it doesn't matter how much money is in your bank account, or how many Rolexes or Mercedes-Benz you have that you've put into your life (water). The impurities of lacking forgiveness remain because what it contains is resentment, anger, and revenge.

Westernized countries operate emotionally and spiritually different from some Asian countries, especially as it pertains to living their life with a foundation of character, virtue and morals. In Western cultures, many are not taught forgiveness, or even how to forgive. Instead, it seems resentment and revenge is the order of the day, becoming angry and blaming others for what happens in our lives instead of taking personal responsibility.

Your circumstances do not define your future. Your decisions do.

Forgiveness is a decision. The world around you does not typically support forgiving yourself and other people. In fact, the opposite is true.

When you begin The Ultimate Life Makeover™, consider the act and choice to forgive. Put it into your awareness that it is not possible to achieve inner peace, joy, happiness and fulfillment while simultaneously being resentful, vengeful and angry with yourself or someone who has or you perceive has wronged you.

Consider it the gift you were given at birth; the gift of forgiveness. People mistakenly believe forgiveness has something to do with another person. Many also believe that forgiving someone who has wronged them lets the offending party off the hook. I'm frequently told, "I will never forgive that person. You don't understand what they've done to me!"

Forgiveness is a gift that you give to yourself.

By forgiving someone, you are not giving it to another. It does not mean what they did is okay. It means that you are on the path to being okay.

The best way to start any life makeover or life growth pattern is to become aware of what holds you back. As soon as you become aware, you can do something about it. Another word for that awareness is consciousness. Most people are wandering around asleep, or not fully awake.

The first part of growth is coming to the conclusion you have issues with forgiveness. Next, determine if your forgiveness issues are directed at other people, and who they are. When you are constantly dwelling on counting the ways you've been wronged, it fosters resentment. If you're steeped in blame and resentment, you will never be happy. Winning the lottery will not make you happy because you can't offset those things with materialism. That is not a replacement for forgiveness.

When I do a presentation surrounding forgiveness, I refer my audiences to my number one resource on forgiveness, Dr. Fred Luskin's book, *Forgive For Good.* This excellent book will lead you down the path of understanding the concept of forgiveness, and how important forgiveness is.

I often work with people who have spent a lifetime punishing themselves for what they perceive others have done to them.

Once you create awareness of who you've been directing anger and resentment towards, you can move forward and do something about it. If you are stuck in quicksand and you ignore it, believing you're not stuck, you'll never be able to get free from it. So creating awareness is an important first step.

It doesn't mean you forget the situation. No, it isn't about forgetting.

It isn't necessary to forget. It's about forgiving. The healthy part is the forgiveness itself.

I have long since forgiven myself for the death of the five-year-old child, but I will never forget it. I also needed to forgive the others involved that they didn't use the crosswalk and crossed in the middle of heavy traffic.

On a much higher level, nothing in life is a coincidence. Nothing happens by accident, and all things have a purpose. Some who are wronged never get over it, living their whole life with the after effects of something that happened long ago, never stopping to consider the benefit of acknowledgement.

Forgiveness often goes back to how you see yourself. Many don't see themselves as worthy of forgiveness and constantly punish themselves for mistakes they've made. Is there really such a thing as a mistake?

Perhaps you really can't make a mistake. Maybe all the things you've considered mistakes are in fact learning tools put in our path purposefully as a "miss take". Once learned, now I can push the reset button and do something different the next time. If someone wrongs me, maybe I had never stopped to consider they do not know any other way to treat me.

We all have an internal balancing system, and it is like a giant debit and credit bank account, managed by your conscious. It acts like the gatekeeper, and every time you go through a life situation where you believe you've been wronged by someone and you hold on to it, you are debiting your account. Every time you take action to forgive the person, you gain a credit to your account.

Consider your life as a giant investment account. Everything you do that is in alignment with forgiveness puts credit in your account. You are allowed to go back and forgive for as long as you can remember. You are also permitted to pay forgiveness forward. You can make a decision now that if in the future someone has betrayed or wronged you, you will forgive that person.

Decide now that you are not going to let people debit your happiness account. You are not going to let them debit your inner peace, your inner joy or your fulfillment.

When you read quality books about personal development, psychologists and therapists will tell you forgiveness is the essence of inner peace. You cannot possibly have inner peace while harboring resentment and hate.

What supports forgiveness in your life? Consider who and what in your life supports the concept of forgiveness. Does what you watch on TV or at the movies support forgiveness? Is it something your peers and closest friends support? What about your work associates or your employer? Do they all support forgiveness, or do they fuel the opposite?

TIME TO TAKE ACTION

Grab your pen and write the names of five people throughout your life that you feel have wronged, harmed or betrayed you in some way. You can prioritize them if you like. If you have forgiveness issues with yourself, write your name on the list.

You have an awareness that choosing not to forgive is self-destructive. For each of the names you have listed, take the time to carefully consider that whatever they have done is because of something that went on inside of them that caused them to take the action they took. It is not because of something inside of you.

When it comes to yourself, you have to identify what it is that you won't let go of and identify why you won't let go of it. It is possible you consciously did something to hurt another; you betrayed someone or took something from them.

On the path of forgiveness, it is not necessary to contact someone to tell them you have forgiven them. Again, forgiveness is not about the other person. If somebody wronged or betrayed you, forgiving them is not about them. It is about you. Forgiveness is something you do internally, for yourself. You are not giving them a gift; you are not letting them off the hook. You are letting yourself off the hook.

If you feel contacting someone to tell them you forgive them will give you fulfillment, go ahead! It is contextual because there's so many forgiveness issues I couldn't even begin to go through 1% of them. You may feel contacting them is necessary in order for you to take the next step toward personal growth, but be aware they may not reciprocate your feelings.

In a situation where you know that you have wronged someone, I recommend you ask for his or her forgiveness. Based on my belief systems, that may even take into account people that have graduated from this lifetime, but go ahead and ask them anyway.

Until you understand that forgiveness of yourself and others is a major life transformation, you cannot transform your life. You will never make over your life into what you've always wanted it to be until you release yourself. Set yourself free.

There is no guarantee that when you ask for their forgiveness that they will forgive you and that is ok. Do you base your life on who likes and does not like you? Or is it based on YOU liking you? That is fundamental to know.

I don't know anybody who hasn't wronged somebody at one time or another. I certainly have in my lifetime, as you now know. I cheated on my wife; I cheated in relationships. I would never do those things again. I have learned to forgive myself and the others involved, even publicly. Once you have the awareness that you have forgiveness issues, then you can move forward.

If you push forgiveness issues to the side and think you will just figure out a way to be happy, you are doing nothing but playing the happiness lottery. That lottery is not going to change a thing, because you cannot buy forgiveness. You practice it.

Now you have begun the journey, The Ultimate Life Makeover™.

CHAPTER 32

STEP 2: THE 24 HOUR TRUTH CHALLENGE

IN THE HAPPINESS FORMULA, THE H STANDS FOR HONESTY. YOU have to be honest with yourself. The T stands for truth; you have to be truthful with other people.

I started my speaking career with a presentation called The Power Of Truth™ because being honest makes you unbelievably internally strong. The challenge you will face when implementing truth and honesty is that your actions become the exception, rather than what has sadly become the norm, being deceptive, lying and withholding.

Globally, it appears we have come to a place where being deceptive or lying is accepted normal behavior in society. There is no shortage of people who have come to me with questions about how they can take their business to the next level with deceptive practices.

It's interesting to me that people will come to me at the end of my presentation about The Power Of Truth, and directly ask for my opinion of lying to take their business to the next level!

Typically, you can never avoid the debit and credit life account I explained in the last chapter. No one has immunity to that. You may think you know somebody that tells thousands of lies and appears to be getting away with it, but no, they are not getting away with it. That is just your *perception.*

Within the nervous system, most people associate pain to being honest, and associate pleasure with avoiding honesty as a quick fix.

Example: Imagine you're four years old and you smell cookies baking in the oven. You walk into the kitchen, see a big plate of cookies, and you take one and eat it. Five minutes later your mother or father says, "Did you take a cookie off that plate?" You answer "Yes". You've told the truth. What happens next?

If those cookies were baked specifically for another, it is likely you will be punished. What's happened is that at four years old, you've potentially made an association that honesty brings pain. It's like getting burned when you touch a hot stove. You learn to avoid touching a hot stove.

A month later, the same thing happens, and you go to the kitchen and take the cookie. When asked, the answer you provide might be "No, I didn't take it" thereby getting short-term gratification from the avoidance of punishment. Where do you draw the line?

I'm told all the time that white lies are ok, but there is no such thing as a white lie. Where did that term come from anyway? I wanted to know so I did some research and discovered it came from someone who practiced cognitive dissonance. That is nothing more than a justification for every lie that's told. There's always a justification for it.

There is no inconsequential lie.

You are either telling the truth or you are telling a lie. When you lie, you are withholding the truth. This is another thing people have a challenge with, thinking withholding the truth is not lying. But if you avoid the truth by withholding it, where do you draw the line?

You are either honest or you are not. The license plate on my vehicle is very thought provoking for a lot of people. As I drive down the street, some people will honk the horn and wave, and sometime they will honk the horn and do something else with their hand. My license plate says: **"DON'T LIE"**.

At the end of the first Power of Truth™ presentation, I gave the audience an action step to take. I can't simply make this about me standing in front of an audience of 300, delivering information about the benefits of being honest and how being honest strengthens your immune system without making it personal for their audience.

I challenged everyone in the room to be completely honest and authentic for the next 24 hours. No exception. No matter what happens, I wanted them to take the challenge and do it. I told them it will bring into their awareness how many lies they tell, and that number will astound them. Doing so would also bring into their awareness of why they are telling those lies, and how many of those lies will now seem ridiculous.

An example of a simple, yet ridiculous lie would be if someone approaches you and says, "You know John Smith, right?" You say, "Yeah, I know John", but you really have no clue who John Smith is. You chose to lie.

Every time you do that, you are debiting your account. You are debiting your inner strength, and your ability to create inner peace, joy, fulfillment and happiness for yourself. The other thing you will notice, is perhaps the center of your chest, your solar plexus feels different. YOU feel different. It isn't just an emotional thing, but it is a physical thing as well.

After the 24-hour challenge has passed, I've had people come to me and tell me, "You know, all I do is tell lies. I don't ever tell the truth." That person was very sad because it brought into their awareness that their life had become one lie on top of the other. When people tell white lies, in a very short period they become color blind.

If you are a white lie teller, where do you draw the line? You don't. You just don't realize you're not drawing the line because it all depends on how much pressure and how much leverage is put on you.

Take this action step for yourself. Take The 24-hour Truth Challenge and see what it reveals.

TIME TO TAKE ACTION

Grab your pen and write lines numbered 1 through 10.

On lines one through five, write the worst lies you have ever told that caused the most damage in your or other people's lives.

On lines six through nine, write four major truths you've withheld when asked a question.

On line 10, write down the very last lie you told.

Again, the purpose of this action step is to bring truth into your awareness. If your goal in life is to be happy, you must be aware that you cannot purchase honesty. You must practice it.

Imagine a life without lies! So many people have told me they believe it is impossible to live without lying, and I suspect most have learned to associate massive pain with being honest. I associate massive pain and potentially dying with telling lies. That is a very different concept.

I believe the reason I had that near death experience is because I lived an incongruent life. When you live an incongruent life long enough, you will run out of credits, and it will all be debits in your account. At that time, I had no more credits left. When you have no more credits left, your immune system crashes. In my case, I was a minute or two from crossing over to the other side.

You cannot understate honesty either. There are many statistics about lying, and some of them are earth shattering. There are statistics that say the average person lies two to three times per ten minutes, and that a vast percentage of people on planet earth lie all the time. There is no shortage of statistics about lying you can find, but the importance is not the statistics. The importance is not *being* the statistic.

If you want to have great relationships, whether that is in love or friendship, those relationships must be based on a foundation of trust. If you tell one lie, you have undermined the trust factor in that relationship. Trust is earned, not given. You cannot purchase trust. You have to earn it, and one lie will ruin it. It is amazing how the smallest lies will ruin years of trust.

Honest businesses don't necessarily make more money than dishonest businesses. Long term, imagine what would happen if the CEO of a worldwide corporation, with 100,000 employees, had an epiphany after taking a 24-hour truth challenge and committed to no longer practice deception as a means of making a profit. The CEO puts out a memo to all 100,000 employees that states:

From this day forward, there will be no more lies of any kind told in this company under any set of circumstances. No lies. No withholding of the truth. No deception. This company is going to operate authentically and honestly from this day forward – without exception.

What would be the future of that company? What is the future of the company you currently work for, assuming that the company that you currently work for doesn't have a rule like that? What's the future of your relationship or relationships based on your choice? It IS a choice to be deceptive, to withhold the truth or to tell white lies.

At some point, you have to make a decision about the value of your life. Is the value of your life going to be based on acquisitions and conquests? Is it going to be based on imbalances? When you get to the end of this journey, the only tangible thing you can take with you is the character, ethics, integrity and morals you have developed while you're here. That's it. You can't take the Rolls Royce, the private jet, the 15,000 square foot house and the bank account. The only way you will develop character is to take action, so go ahead. Write out the answers to the above list, and take the challenge.

Now, I could have stood in front of that first audience years ago and said, "I challenge everybody in here to be completely honest and authentic for the rest of their life." What are the chances anyone would attempt that challenge? It would be highly unlikely, but anybody can do it for 24 hours.

I have 15 years of experience with this particular challenge, and I frequently receive emails from people I haven't seen in years. The common thread of those emails is "I want you to know the presentation you did and the 24-hour Challenge changed my life for the better, from that day forward to today; for myself and for the lives of the people around me."

Consider what you want out of your life. Consider your dreams. Consider your own pursuit of happiness. Consider how you're going to get there, because you do not want to get to the end of this journey and say, "I wish I would have told the truth."

"One who lies to himself, and believes his own lies, becomes unable to recognize truth, either in himself or in anyone else, and he ends up losing respect for himself and for others. When he has no respect for anyone, he can no longer love, and in him, he yields to his impulses, indulges in the lowest form of pleasure, and behaves in the end like an animal in satisfying his vices. And it all comes from lying - to others and to yourself."

– Fyodor Dostoyevsky, The Brothers Karamazov

CHAPTER 33

STEP 3: SELF-WORTH

THE ELEMENTS OF THE HAPPINESS FORMULA ARE NOT FOR SALE online, in your local market or at the mall. You have to practice them.

These elements are critical to living a balanced life. If you don't practice all three of the elements of the formula, your life is going to be unbalanced, and become so that it would be impossible to feel happiness. If you practice suppression and repression of emotions, you will never be able to get there.

Self-Worth is the third element of the happiness formula. If you lack self-worth, are you able to give yourself the gift of forgiveness? It is unlikely. If you lack self-worth, will you be able to be honest? Also unlikely.

These three elements complement each other and work together. People have thought I left gratitude out of the formula, but I did not forget it. Gratitude, compassion, empathy...all of these are part of self-worth. If you practice self-worth, you are also practicing gratitude, empathy and random acts of kindness. When you treat other people the way you like to be treated, that is all part of self-worth.

If you grew up like I did with an inferiority complex. If you feel inferior to other people, and compare yourself to other people, stop. It's not a healthy practice.

In school, had I been asked to write a list of ten traits of low self-worth and ten traits of healthy self-worth, I would have only been able to compile one list. I never knew the traits of someone with a healthy self-worth. How can you practice something when you don't even know what it is?

There is no substitute for self-worth. You cannot substitute ego; that is the opposite of self-worth. You cannot substitute materialism for self-worth. You cannot substitute things for self-worth. Self-worth is self-worth.

How do you develop self-worth? The first thing you have to do is understand what the traits of self-worth are. Below is a list of 21 traits; there are more, but these are the basics.

21 TRAITS OF HIGH SELF WORTH PEOPLE

- [ ] They set boundaries and respect others boundaries.
- [ ] They do not need or thrive on validation and praise.
- [ ] They do not have issues with rejection, criticism or blame.
- [ ] They avoid manipulation and guilt by others.
- [ ] They tend to live in the present moment.
- [ ] They get personal satisfaction and fulfillment from hobbies and work achievements.
- [ ] They have healthy communication skills; they listen to understand, rather than respond.
- [ ] They have an internal sense; they are enough and clearly understand their worth.
- [ ] They have a clear path when it comes to virtues and values.
- [ ] They have no fear of self-expression and take full responsibility for their actions.
- [ ] They have no fear of intimacy.

- ❑ Self-care is a primary life path; they avoid being a pleaser or rescuer.
- ❑ They continue to grow into consciousness and awareness.
- ❑ They never compare themselves to others, financially, physically or intelligently.
- ❑ They are in control of their life. They say no when they mean no, and say yes when they mean yes.
- ❑ They tend to create balance with everything that comes their way, good or bad.
- ❑ They have a clear understanding that emotions and feelings are natural, and they tend to avoid using their imagination to add negative feelings to the emotions.
- ❑ They DO NOT care what others think about them.
- ❑ Rejection is a gift, NOT a punishment.
- ❑ They understand that love can be a misused word that means "I Want or Need" what you can give me.
- ❑ They know it is essential to unconditionally love themselves.

Self-worth will shift the quality of your life dramatically.

A resource I highly commend is a book called, *Ten Days to Self-Esteem*, by David D. Burns.

The goal of achieving self-worth is to discover an unconditional love for yourself. There is nobody like you on planet earth. You are not supposed to look like other people. You are unique to you. You aren't here to earn the love of other people. You came here to love yourself and love other people.

There is no substitute for self-worth. Self-worth will dramatically change everything about your life. Let me share some things that will change:

Healthy self-esteem will change the quality of your health because it strengthens your constitution, your inner strength.

You will understand, respect and create boundaries for yourself that you won't deviate from, and will learn to avoid those who don't. There will be those who will attempt to run over you, and back up to see what they've hit but with those boundaries in place, the damage will be minimal.

TIME TO TAKE ACTION

Review the above list of **21 Traits of High Self-Worth People.**

Starting with the first trait on the list, each day for the next 21 days, I want you to focus on that one trait throughout the day; bring it into your awareness.

Consider what that trait is, what it means to you, and how it applies to your life in a positive or negative way.

Write down (no really, write it down) your thoughts on whether this trait is one you have mastered or need to put forth additional focus to resolve. Then write down what your first step will be to resolve the issue with that trait. At the end of the day, check it off as complete.

You will walk through life very differently when you have deemed having a healthy self-worth a priority. You will discover forgiving people becomes instantaneous. Being honest with yourself and others becomes effortless. This does not mean you will not have issues around being honest. It just means that along with the issues you will still be honest.

People respect others who are honest, and those who are honest possess healthy self-respect. Remember that every lie you tell debits your account, and when you keep debiting your account, you are debiting self-respect.

Remember, your circumstances do not dictate your future. I have certainly listed enough of my own personal circumstances in this book that appeared to be insurmountable. They should have caused learned helplessness and learned hopelessness, but the opposite occurred. That is my main purpose of sharing this material: It would be so easy to fall into the hole of learned helplessness and learned hopelessness, but when you achieve healthy self-worth you will never have cause to go there. What has happened or what will happen to you will not deter you from climbing any mountain you choose.

The Happiness Formula™ is simple and powerful, and the elements go back thousands of years. It is the solution to finding your true purpose in life. Most likely, you will discover your purpose will find you.

Conclusion

I heard a story years ago, and though I do not recall its origin, I remember its value. It gives clarity, meaning and depth to the content of this book and I want to share it with you:

One day a young man was feeling like a lost soul. His marriage was falling apart, he was suffering financially and was in overwhelming debt. He questioned his reason for living, and decided to take a walk on the beach to contemplate his fate.

As he walked, he came upon an old man sitting in the sand and staring at the surf. As he passed, the old man stopped him and asked why he looked so sad. The young man replied, "My life is a mess. My wife is leaving me. I'm emotionally, spiritually and financially broke." The old man said, "I know what that feels like. I am 88 years old and just lost my wife of 60 years. It is really difficult."

The old man made an offer to help the young man, telling him he would give him the chance to win $500 by challenging him to a foot race down the beach.

The young man had no access to the $500 to enter into the bet, and did not comprehend the obvious advantage he had based on the age difference. Sadly, he told the old man he didn't have a way to raise the bet money, and declined the old man's help.

The old man said, "If you change your mind and want me to help you, I am here every day." The young man wandered off.

Several days later, the young man returned, having scraped up the $500 needed to cover the bet. He said, "Ok, old man. Let's get this over with."

The old man stood up to get ready to run, but stopped and said to the young man, "Wait a minute. You need to turn around and run backward." The young man was shocked, saying, "Wait a minute! What do you mean I have to run backward?" The old man replied, "We just need to even the odds. I am an old man, and you are a strong, young man."

The young man agreed and turned around, preparing to begin the race. The old man spoke again, saying, "Oh, you also need to put your feet in this burlap sack, and tie the top of the sack around your waist." The young man was getting very irritated, but agreed based on the old man's claim of having the greater advantage.

Once again, they got ready to start when the old man made one more request. "You need to be blindfolded." The young man, now very angry, demanded a valid reason from the old man for this additional request. The old man told him, "Once again, you still have a huge advantage over me." The young man desperately needed the $500 prize, so he agreed.

The old man yelled, "GO!" and down the beach they ran. The outcome displeased the young man, because the old man did in fact win the race.

The young man was beyond angry at the old man for taking advantage of him, when the old man claimed to want to help him.

The old man sat him down and told him, "I have now taught you a great life lesson that took me my whole life to learn." Confused, the young man asked what that life lesson was.

Calmly, the old man asked the younger, "Do you know why I won?"

The young man said, "Well, I think you cheated me."

The old man quickly responded, "NOT true! The reason I won is simple. You allowed me to make all the rules, and I made the rules so that I could not lose."

Who have you allowed to make all the rules in your life, and create your beliefs? Your parents? Your teachers? Your friends? Your significant others? Your Employers? Your religion? Your peers?

Are all those rules and beliefs designed so that you would win and be happy, healthy and emotionally balanced? Or were they designed not to be in your favor?

Many people possess values and live by rules that prevent them from having any possible chance of being happy and experiencing any form of inner peace. They wait for something good to happen to them. They chase after something or someone that will bring them short-term gratification that temporarily satisfies them until they find another object that will fill the hollow place in the mind and heart.

In looking back at my life and in the lives of those I have interviewed, I have found nearly everyone in some form or another has left the rules up to others to define. I've asked the question thousands of times, "What are you trying to make happen in your life?", and invariably the answer is almost always, "I just want to be successful." On three occasions, the answer was "I want to be happy."

In my presentations, I will often teach by teaching "The Unhappiness Formula", the "Ultimate Life Mess", by pointing out that one must stop doing what makes them unhappy.

If you truly want to be happy, healthy, rich and balanced:

- Speak from your heart.
- Share how you really feel.

- Embrace suffering rather than hide from it.
- Seek not the comfort zone, for it is really the decay zone.
- Add value to everyone's path you cross, expecting nothing in return.
- Understand and work with the laws of the universe, rather than against them.
- Above all else, make your own rules to be Honest, Forgiving and practice the traits of healthy Self-Worth every day of the rest of your precious life.

In creating and practicing The Happiness Formula™, and with much reflection, introspection, guidance from brilliant therapists, amazing support from true friends, I am finally emotionally free.

To be emotionally free is THE Ultimate Life Makeover. I wish the same for YOU.

I live on an island in the Gulf of Mexico called Paradise Island, connected by a series of bridges to the mainland.

The Bridge Builder

An old man going a lone highway,
Came, at the evening cold and gray,
To a chasm vast and deep and wide.
Through which was flowing a sullen tide
The old man crossed in the twilight dim,
The sullen stream had no fear for him;
But he turned when safe on the other side
And built a bridge to span the tide.

"Old man," said a fellow pilgrim near,
"You are wasting your strength with building here;

Your journey will end with the ending day,
You never again will pass this way;
You've crossed the chasm, deep and wide,
Why build this bridge at evening tide?"

The builder lifted his old gray head;
"Good friend, in the path I have come," he said,
"There followed after me to-day
A youth whose feet must pass this way.
This chasm that has been as naught to me
To that fair-haired youth may a pitfall be;
He, too, must cross in the twilight dim;
Good friend, I am building this bridge for him!"

By: Will Allen Dromgoole

The purpose is to build the bridge of a happy healthy life for you and yours.

Gary King

The Happiness Formula
Is based on honesty and authenticity
Recognizing that every lie has consequences
and happiness only grows from the
Certainty of Truth.

The Happiness Formula
Is built of a foundation of self-worth,
Which is the core of all human life,
Knowing that true wisdom
Requires self-care.

Be forgiving
Be honest
Be truthful
Be worthy of yourself
Be happy ...

By: Vickie H. Smith

About The Author

Gary King is a speaker, author, and successful entrepreneur. His background is diverse and exhilarating including professional powerboat racing; internationally known artist and sculptor, honored by President Clinton; and General Manager and Vice president of sales and marketing in the television industry.

Gary has successfully owned and operated King Marine Engineering since 1972 adding King Productions International in 1981. He is an expert in event production and logistics producing and directing some of the largest motor sports events in the Tampa Bay area including the 2001 APBA Offshore Powerboat World Championships.

Along with his personal company accomplishments, Gary contracted as Director of Security, Road Manager, Operations Manager and consultant to Anthony Robbins and Robbins Research International for the over 25 years.

Over the last 15 years at global events, Gary passionately developed a profound message and travels globally six months each year to share his message with leaders and entrepreneurs, in schools, prisons, and to teen groups. His message is timely and riveting on the subject of Character, Ethics, Integrity and Forgiveness. His message has appeared in articles in Oprah Magazine, O's Guide to Life, Positive Impact magazine and has had numerous articles published related to, Character is our Bailout.

Gary's life story is filled with amazing accomplishments and honors, and many unthinkable nightmares, yet he ventures forward with the heart and soul of a victor.

Gary's messages, branded and trademarked as The Power of Truth™, The Happiness Formula® and The Ultimate Life Makeover™, have dramatically enhanced the lives of thousands of people in many cultures.

Gary is passionate about bringing the United States and the World, back to a foundation of Self-Worth, Character and Integrity starting with the public schools, and helping returning veterans rise above the overwhelming challenges of PTSD. He has also created a non-profit foundation to serve those that are without resources and in need of emotional support.

Gary King is truly a Renaissance man.

Resources

Visit www.GaryKingLive.com

- The 24 Hour Truth Challenge
- The 24 Hour Forgiveness Challenge
- The 21 Day Self Worth Challenge

Additional programs, videos and event announcements at www.GaryKingLive.com

Visit with Gary via Facebook : www.Facebook.com/GaryKingLive

Ghostwriting and editing:

Vickie Smith, Certified High Performance Coach

www.TheBigIdeaStrategist.com

Lisa Morgan, Online Business Manager

www.VirtuosoBusinessSolutions.com

Books Referenced

The Psychopath Next Door by Martha Stout

I Hate You, Don't Leave Me by Jerold J. Kreisman, M.D. and Hal Strauss

Getting Past The Past by Francine Shapiro

Dying To Be Me by Anita Moorjanis

Forgive for Good, by Dr. Fred Luskin

The 10 Steps to Self Esteem, by David Burns

Just Be Honest, by Steven Gaffney

Think and Grow Rich by Napoleon Hill

Video Referenced

Do Schools Kill Creativity by Sir Ken Robinson

Sources

[1]PTSD - The Statistics. (n.d.). Retrieved 2016, from PTSD Foundation of America: http://ptsdusa.org/what-is-ptsd/the-statistics/

[2]Personal Development Industry - Melanie Lindner, What People Are Still Willing To Pay For

1/15/2009 - http://www.forbes.com/2009/01/15/self-help-industry-ent-sales-cx_ml_0115selfhelp.html

CPSIA information can be obtained
at www.ICGtesting.com
Printed in the USA
FFOW02n1324110617
36568FF